S0-BFD-449

Midwest Moms

Recipes & Advice from the Heartland

Midwest Moms

Recipes & Advice

from the Heartland

Linda Nolan Polly

1-12-08

COPYRIGHT © 2007 BY LINDA NOLAN POLLY
www.midwestmomscookbook.com

PHOTOGRAPHY COPYRIGHTS:
  Shutterstock.com
  Randy Edmonds Photography ~ Lawrence, Kansas
    www.randyedmondsphotography.com
  Josh Zuckerman Photography ~ New York, New York
    www.jzphoto.com
  Polly Family Archive

LIBRARY OF CONGRESS
CATALOGING-IN-PUBLICATION DATA:
ISBN 978-0-615-16937-8
Polly, Linda Nolan
  Midwest Moms: Recipes and Advice from the Heartland

BOOK DESIGN:
Lawson Phillips Associates ~ Topeka, Kansas
  Lawson Phillips
  Arthur McCash
  Garet Phillips

Printed in Mexico by RR Donnelley

Table of Contents

Table of Contents

Foreword

I WAS FORTUNATE while growing up to live half my childhood in rural Iowa on one of the family farms and the other half nearby in the small town of Guthrie Center. Cooking, baking, and family meals went hand in hand with parenting opportunities. We still farm the land in Iowa and South Dakota where these same family values continue today.

This collection of easy to prepare recipes and advice was gathered from my friends who live in Kansas, Iowa, South Dakota, Missouri, Michigan, Minnesota, and Illinois. This book combines tested recipes and equally well tested advice. Many of the women I admire most have contributed to this book.

There is no better place to raise a family than the Midwest. I know. I've lived in many cities in the US and Europe, and the heartland is where we chose to raise our family.

*

My thanks to my two grown children, Matthew and Shannon, who made parenting easy and who are now my teachers, their father and my husband of forty years, Dr. Richard Polly, and our son-in-law, Garry Reeder, all of whom give my life purpose.

*

Many parenting skills are passed from one generation to another. My parents, John and Florence Nolan (both deceased), gave every day of their lives to hard work and a total commitment to their four children. My best friends growing up were my sister and two brothers, Dr. Sheila Town, and Mark and Bill Nolan, and they still are. My life has been enriched by my sister-in-law, Jenny Nolan, Linda and Dick Brown and Dr. Marla Geha.

*

I am in debt to my creative designers, Lawson Phillips and Arthur McCash of Lawson Phillips Associates, whose tenacity kept this project on target. Garet Phillips gave a feminine perspective and proofread.

*

Recipes were contributed by Kansas Governor Kathleen Sebelius, Gladys Nolan Corcoran (deceased), Dori Murphy, Bev Menninger, Bette Donahey, Nancy Perry, Susan Horan Garlinghouse, Dorothy Prager, Julie Douthett, Betty Cleland, Jana Barry, Cindy Giessel, Janet McElroy, Marilyn Ward, Dorothy Fager, Paula Baum, Paula O'Callaghan, Shirley Hobbs, Barbara Riessen, Teresa O'Neal, Judyanne Somers, Carole Etzel, Adabelle Haughawout, Debbie Spees, Paula Peterson, Terry Schwartz, Beth Fager, Kansas State Senator Alicia Salisbury, Deana Beardmore, Widge Yager, Jean Ramberg, Penny Lumpkin, Mary Alice McRae, Joan Tempero, Sherry Wieck, Nancy Kindling, Bette Bossler, Leah Gabler-Marshall, Florence Nolan (deceased), Jo Halley, Mary Andersen, Nancy Alexander, Pat Reymond, Jeanne Elder, Diana Joliff, Joyce Alberg, Ines Gilbert, Ann Rolley, Pam Ferrell, Mary Hutchinson, Pat Darnall, Donna Adams, Angie Gleason, Marjorie Schnacke (deceased), Shirley Waugh, former First Lady of Kansas Patty Hayden, Marilyn Unrein, Carol Bonebrake,

Karen Welch, Diane Goheen, Mary Martell, Sarah Bailey, Darlene Payne, Ann Borel, Kristin Chanay, Lori Hutchinson, Marge Petty, Mare Czyzewski-Rockefeller, Shirley Henson, Shirley Hobbs, Virginia Reinking, Karen Trobough, Mary Powell Yorke, Linda VandeGarde, Jan Kobach, Belinda McPherson, Brenda Zimmerman, Diane Sneed, Carla Hutton, Bobbi Showalter, and Jane Boldenow.

*

Advice was contributed by Kansas Governor Kathleen Sebelius, Nancy Alexander, Marilyn Unrein, Linda VandeGarde, Kristin Chanay, Jana Barry, Sharon Wieck, Diane Goheen, Mary Alice McRae, Betty Cleland, Widge Yager, Leah Gabler-Marshall, Nancy Kindling, Jo Halley, Paula Baum, Deana Beardmore, Diana Joliff, Brenda Clark, Linda Marling, Pam Ferrell, Pat Darnall, Janet McElroy, Barb Riessen, Sarah Bailey, Paula O'Callaghan, Pat Reymond, Dori Murphy, Bette Donahey, Debbie Spees, Kansas State Senator Alicia Salisbury, Susan Horan Garlinghouse, Mary Powell Yorke, Carol Bonebrake, Teresa O'Neal, Mary Martell, Diane Sneed, Penny Lumpkin, Jane Boldenow, Meredith Williams, Carole Etzel, Terry Schwartz, Cindy Giessel, Mare Czyzewski-Rockefeller, Ines Gilbert, Helen Crow, Bev Menninger, Beth Trimble Burnett, Julie Douthett, Kansas State Representative Lana Gordon, Rene Smith, Donna Adams, Katy Franklin, Mary Dorsey Wanless, Jan Benson, and a tribute to Dorothy Fager.

May you enjoy the recipes, wisdom, and humor of my good friends.

Linda Polly

Linda Polly
Topeka, Kansas
December, 2007

Introduction

GIVING IS RECEIVING. Like many mothers I know, I was more than a little concerned when my son decided he had to have a dog. I knew who was going to have to take care of it, and I already believed I had my hands full with two children. But his father wanted our son to have a complete childhood so I was out-voted. Our son read all the dog books, selected the breed, and rode off to Kansas City with his dad to pick out the "perfect" dog. And he did. Late that evening they came home with a frightened, two-month-old Shetland Sheepdog sick from his first car ride. Our son slept on the kitchen floor all that first night with "Tex" (Matthew was a fanatical Dallas Cowboys fan). Tex stole our hearts, especially mine. He always looked at me and listened when I talked, and he never talked back. He was always waiting at the door anxious to see me every time I came home, and he slept at my feet when I was sick. About whom can you say as much? Yes, he chewed up an expensive drapery; he occasionally got sick on the rug; he ran out of the open backyard gate every time we forgot to close it; and the vet bills were significant. But it was the best decision dad and son ever made. Eventually, the kids grew up and went off to college. Dad spent the usual long hours at work, but Tex was always with me... until, he wasn't. It broke my heart the day this 15-year-old Sheltie was put to sleep. I held him in my arms as he died, carried him home, had a "funeral" alone, and buried him on the side of the yard where I can still talk to him. No one but Tex knows that I do. Sometimes I still look up and think for a fleeting moment that he has gotten up from his favorite spot atop the air conditioning vent, padded over to the kitchen, and peeked around the counter just to check on me. Now he is only in my heart. So...we gave our son the gift of a pet, but in the end he really gave the gift to me. LINDA POLLY

APPETIZERS APPETIZERS APPETIZERS APPETIZERS APPETIZERS APPETIZERS APPETIZERS APPETIZERS APPET

Appetizers

Appetizers Appetizers Appetizers Appetizers Appetizers Appetizers Appetizers Appetizers Appetizers Appetizers Appetizers Appetizers Appetizers Appetizers Appetizers Appetizers Appetizers Appetizers Appetizers

APRICOT BRIE

INGREDIENTS
1 c. apricot preserves
3/4 c. brandy
One 2 lb. Brie cheese wheel

DIRECTIONS
…Place Brie on serving tray.
…Poke holes in the top of cheese.
…Heat the preserves and brandy until hot, but not boiling.
…Pour over cheese.

ARTICHOKE DIP

INGREDIENTS
1 can artichoke hearts, drained
1/2 c. mayonnaise
3/4 c. Parmesan cheese
1 small can chopped green chilies
Grated cheddar cheese

DIRECTIONS
…Combine artichoke hearts, mayonnaise, Parmesan cheese, and chilies.
…Pour into 9 inch greased baking dish.
…Top with grated cheese.
…Bake at 350 degrees for 20 to 25 minutes.
…Serve with crackers.

ARTICHOKE SQUARES

INGREDIENTS
6 oz. marinated artichoke hearts
1 small onion, finely chopped
4 eggs, beaten
12 small square saltine crackers
1/2 lb. sharp cheddar cheese, grated

DIRECTIONS
…Drain artichoke hearts, save marinade.
…Sauté onion in artichoke marinade.
…Drain.
…Combine onion with artichokes.
…Add eggs, crushed crackers, and cheese.
…Mix well.
…Pour into greased 8 inch baking dish.
…Bake at 325 degrees for 35 to 40 minutes.
…Cut into squares and serve.

ASPARAGUS FINGERS

INGREDIENTS

1/4 c. blue cheese
Two 8 oz. packages cream cheese
2 eggs
2 large loaves white bread
3/4 lb. melted butter
2 cans asparagus

DIRECTIONS

…Mix blue cheese, cream cheese, and eggs together.
…Remove crusts from bread and roll flat.
…Spread with cheese mixture, add an asparagus, and roll up like a jelly roll.
…Pinch end to hold bread in place.
…Dip in butter and place seam side down.
…Bake at 400 degrees for 15 minutes or until bread is golden brown.

BACON WRAPPED DATES

INGREDIENTS

1/2 lb. bacon, cut into thirds
8 oz. box of pitted dates
4 oz. bag of almonds

DIRECTIONS

…Stuff an almond into the middle of each date.
…Wrap each date with bacon, allowing it to overlap.
…Secure with toothpicks.
…Place on cookie sheet.
…Do not let them touch.
…Bake at 400 degrees for 15 to 20 minutes.
…Watch closely so bacon is cooked, but not burned.

BLACK BEAN CHICKEN APPETIZER

INGREDIENTS

1 can black beans, rinsed and drained
12 oz. grated Colby Jack cheese
1 package creamed spinach, thawed
1 jar medium flavored salsa
1 large can white chunk chicken, rinsed and drained

DIRECTIONS

…Mix beans, cheese, spinach, salsa, and chicken.
…Pour into a shallow ovenproof baking dish.
…Bake at 350 degrees for 30 minutes.
…Serve with dipper chips.

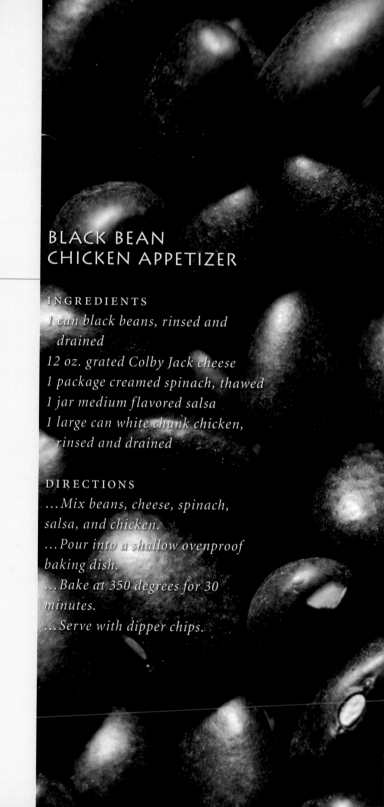

BLACK BEAN SALSA

INGREDIENTS
Two 15 oz. cans black beans, drained
One 16 oz. can medium picante sauce
One 4 oz. can diced green chilies
1/2 c. onion, finely chopped
1 c. corn, optional
1 to 2 cloves fresh garlic, minced
2 Tbsp. fresh lemon juice
1/4 to 1/2 c. fresh cilantro, minced
Salt and fresh ground black pepper

DIRECTIONS
…Combine all ingredients in a bowl.
…Chill 2 hours.
…Serve with tortilla chips, burritos, enchiladas, or grilled chicken.

BROCCOLI DIP

INGREDIENTS
One 10 oz. package chopped broccoli, cooked
1 roll garlic cheese
1 can cream of mushroom soup
One 8 oz. jar sliced mushrooms
1/4 tsp. garlic powder
1/4 c. dry white wine

DIRECTIONS
…Melt cheese with soup.
…Add wine, garlic powder, broccoli, and mushrooms.
…Serve warm in chafing dish with toast rounds.
…Double the recipe for a large chafing dish.

CHISHOLM TRAIL GUACAMOLE DIP

INGREDIENTS
6 avocados
1/2 c. onion, diced
1 c. tomato, chopped
1/4 c. lemon juice
1/2 c. mayonnaise
1/4 c. cilantro
1/2 tsp. garlic salt

DIRECTIONS
…Mash avocados until just chunky.
…Add all other ingredients and mix.
…Cover and seal with plastic wrap so dip does not discolor.
…Refrigerate until serving time.

BAKSHEESH ~ Call them incentives or rewards if you like, but the fact is bribery works. Over the years I have found that when reasoning fails, when persuasive words fall on deaf ears, when raising my voice only raises resistance, a well-targeted bribe never fails to do the trick. Of course, the perceived value of the bribe has to be increased, the harder the task and the older the child. But it is important to remember that with children, money is not everything. A few M&Ms might get you a dry diaper or finished vegetables. The keys to dad's new car might be the key to three hours of yard work. I try to be inventive. I know my children, and I know what they want.

Kansas Governor KATHLEEN SEBELIUS

DON'T FORGET YOURSELF ~ Make time for your own recreation and personal growth. The job of a working mom, whether in an office or at home, typically is hectic and demanding. Making time for yourself may strike you as selfish, if not impossible; but think of it as an investment in your personal well-being and that of your family. How you do it is up to you, but never forget that an evening with dad — and without the kids — is crucial to the happiness of your family.

Kansas State Senator ALICIA SALISBURY

CHUCK DIP

INGREDIENTS

1 1/2 lb. ground chuck
4 whole banana peppers
1 large tomato
1 lb. English or American cheese
Corn or tortilla chips
1 large onion

DIRECTIONS

…Chop the banana peppers and tomato and set aside.
…Dice onion.
…Cut cheese into cubes.
…In a large skillet, brown ground chuck.
…Drain.
…Add onion and cook until tender.
…Add the banana peppers and tomato.
…Heat thoroughly.
…Lower heat.
…Add cheese cubes and stir until melted.
…(Cheese may also be melted in a microwave or double boiler.)
…Spoon mixture into small crock pot and heat on low.
…Serve with chips.

CHUTNEY CHEESE

INGREDIENTS

8 oz. cream cheese, softened
4 oz. sharp cheddar cheese, grated
3/4 tsp. curry powder
3 Tbsp. sherry
1/2 c. chutney
2 chopped scallions, including tops
Salt to taste

DIRECTIONS

…Cream two cheeses.
…Add salt, curry, and sherry.
…Spread 1/2 inch thick on a serving dish.
…Chill until hard.
…Spread chutney on top and sprinkle chopped onions over the top.
…Serve with crackers.

CRAB CRISPS 1

INGREDIENTS

8 oz. crab, drained and chopped
8 oz. grated cheddar cheese
2 Tbsp. chopped scallions
2 Tbsp. chopped mushrooms
Softened butter
English muffins

DIRECTIONS

…Mix crab, cheese, scallions, and mushrooms.
…Add enough butter to bind the mixture.
…Spread on split, toasted English muffin.
…Cut into quarters and broil until cheese melts.

CHILD CONSERVE (A RECIPE) ~ Select a small child and brush him carefully to rid him of any tears. Be careful not to beat as you would an egg or cream, for beating will make him tough and apt to froth at the mouth.

Lift him gently into the home-preserving kettle and tie him with strong cords of affection which are not easily broken. Do not sear him with sarcasm, for that causes sputtering which may ultimately result in spontaneous combustion. Scramble when difficulties arise.

Do not soak him in liquor, for excessive drinking will make him mushy. It is best to let him simmer tenderly, blending gently with delicate seasonings. Stuff him one hour before taking him out or asking him to follow instructions.

Flavor him with the oil of happiness, an ounce of understanding, and a bushel of fun and laughter. Do not spoil him by over-indulgence, but serve him daily on a platter of strength and courage, garnished with kisses and hugs. PENNY LUMPKIN

CRAB CRISPS 2

INGREDIENTS
One 6 1/2 oz. can crab, drained
  and flaked
8 oz. cream cheese
1/2 c. Swiss cheese, shredded
2 Tbsp. onion soup mix
3 dz. Melba toast rounds

DIRECTIONS
…Combine all ingredients
and spread on toast rounds.
…Broil until cheese melts.

THE POTTY DANCE ~ Having the good fortune not only to be a mother but also a grandmother, I have learned that there are some lessons grandmothers are particularly good at teaching children. For example: potty training. The key to "Grandma Potty Training" is a willingness to look foolish. Grandma must make up a really silly dance, which is called "The Grandma Dance." Grandma does the dance ONLY when the child is successful on the potty, but Grandma must do the dance EVERY time success is achieved. The only exception is the "Grandma Poopy Dance," which is done only if the child is successful in that area. While these dances are usually performed in front of a live audience, they can also be done over the phone in cases of emergency. The Grandma Dance is guaranteed to achieve the desired results within three days or your money back. Side effects include a child who won't stop asking Grandma to do the dances long after potty control has been achieved. BETTE DONAHEY

CREAM CHEESE PIZZA DIP

INGREDIENTS
2 packages 8 oz. cream cheese, softened
1 jar chili sauce
1 medium white onion
1 small jar pimientos
1 large green pepper
Chopped black olives
2 c. shredded mozzarella cheese

DIRECTIONS
…Spread cream cheese evenly over a pizza pan or serving tray.
…Spread chili sauce over cream cheese.
…Mince onion and green pepper.
…Drain pimientos and olives.
…Layer these ingredients on pizza.
…Sprinkle with mozzarella cheese.
…Refrigerate overnight.
…Set out one hour before serving.
…Serve with large corn chips.

ELEGANT CAVIAR

INGREDIENTS
5 hard boiled eggs, chopped
3 Tbsp. butter, softened
1 Tbsp. mayonnaise
8 oz. cream cheese, softened
4 green scallions including
  tops, chopped
1 small jar caviar

DIRECTIONS
…Mix eggs, butter, and
mayonnaise.
…Spread onto serving platter in
a circle.
…Chill.
…Mix onions and cream
cheese and spread on top of egg
mixture.
…Spread caviar on top and chill
again.
…Serve with Melba toast
rounds.

ENGLISH MUFFIN CANAPÉS

INGREDIENTS
One 8 oz. package cream cheese
One 4 oz. can crabmeat
1/2 c. butter
1/4 c. grated onion
6 English muffins

DIRECTIONS
…Bring cream cheese and butter to
room temperature.
…Beat with mixer until well blended.
…Add crabmeat and onion and heat.
…Split English muffins and spread
with mixture.
…Cut muffins in quarters.
…Place on cookie sheet and broil
until brown.

ESCARGOT PROSCIUTTO

INGREDIENTS
1 (24 count) can of snails
24 slices prosciutto
1 1/3 c. butter
1 tsp. garlic, minced
1 tsp. lemon juice
1 tsp. white wine
1 tsp. parsley, minced
White pepper

DIRECTIONS
…Rinse and drain snails.
…Roll each snail in a slice
of prosciutto and secure with
toothpick.
…Arrange neatly in chafing dish in
which they will be served.
…Warm snails just before serving.
…Melt butter and garlic and add
lemon juice, wine, pepper, and
parsley immediately before serving.
…Pour over snails in chafing dish.

FIVE-MINUTE MEXICAN DIP

INGREDIENTS

8 oz. cream cheese
1 can chili (no beans)
1 can chopped green chilies
4 oz. grated cheddar cheese

DIRECTIONS

…Spread cream cheese in quiche or other baking dish.
…Cover with chili, green chilies, and cheese.
…Bake at 325 degrees for 20 minutes or until hot in the center.
…Serve with sturdy chips.

GRILLED ASPARAGUS WRAPS

INGREDIENTS

1/2 c. instant couscous
Salt and pepper
2 Tbsp. lemon zest
2 tsp. thyme, chopped
1/2 c. mayonnaise
1 lb. fresh asparagus
Olive oil
1/2 onion, cut in 1/4 inch slices
Four 8 inch tortillas
1 small head red leaf lettuce
3 Tbsp. fresh lemon juice

DIRECTIONS

…Heat grill until hot.
…Boil 3/4 c. water.
…Add couscous and pinch of salt.
…Stir and cover.
…Remove from heat and let stand 5 minutes.
…Fluff with a fork.
…Combine lemon zest, lemon juice, couscous, thyme, and mayonnaise in a bowl.
…Season with salt and pepper.
…Set aside.
…Snap off tough ends of asparagus.
…Toss asparagus and onion slices with a little olive oil.
…Grill seasoned asparagus and onion in a grill basket, turning as needed until spears are slightly charred and round ends soft and brown, about 10 minutes.
…Spread 1/4 of couscous over each tortilla.
…Place 4 asparagus spears over couscous.
…Top with 1/4th of onion and lettuce leaf.
…Roll tightly and serve.
Makes 4 wraps.

ADOPTION ~ Our family was formed through adoption. Our son Hunter is fourteen, and our daughter Chloe is nine. They were blessed with two mothers: one who gave them life, and one who gave them a name. Each child has a book I created especially for them that tells the story of how they became a part of our family. So at the age of five when asked if he knew what a miracle was, Hunter replied, "When a newborn baby comes to live at your house!"

DEBBIE SPEES

HOLIDAY SCALLOPED OYSTERS

INGREDIENTS
1 qt. oysters
2 c. crushed saltine crackers
Butter
Salt and pepper
1 egg
1/2 c. milk

DIRECTIONS
…Preheat oven to 350 degrees.
…Drain oysters, reserving liquid.
…Alternate layers of cracker crumbs and oysters in a buttered casserole.
…Dot each layer with butter and season with salt and pepper until all ingredients are in casserole.
…Beat the egg with the milk.
…Add oyster liquid.
…Pour over casserole.
…Bake uncovered for 30 minutes.

HOT ARTICHOKE DIP

INGREDIENTS
One 8 oz. jar artichoke hearts
1 c. real mayonnaise
1 c. Parmesan cheese

DIRECTIONS
…Drain artichoke hearts and mash.
…Drain off all liquid.
…Blend artichokes, mayonnaise and cheese in bowl until smooth.
…Pour into ovenproof glass dish.
…Bake at 425 degrees for 15 to 20 minutes until top is browned.
…Serve with tortilla chips.

HOT CRAB DIP

INGREDIENTS
1 lb. crabmeat
16 oz. cream cheese, softened
2 small onions, finely chopped
2 Tbsp. sherry
1/2 c. sliced almonds

DIRECTIONS
…Mix all ingredients except
almonds.
…Pour into shallow casserole.
…Top with almonds.
…Bake at 350 degrees for 25
minutes or until hot in the center.
…Serve immediately with
crackers.

HOT CRABMEAT DIP

INGREDIENTS
One 8 oz. package cream cheese
1/2 c. butter
1 small onion, finely chopped
4 dashes Tabasco sauce
1 clove garlic, minced
16 oz. white crabmeat, thawed and
  well drained

DIRECTIONS
…Melt cream cheese and butter in a
double boiler.
…Stir in onion, seasonings, and garlic.
…Add crabmeat.
…Mix thoroughly and heat.
…Serve hot in chafing dish.
(This may be served on phyllo pastry
squares, pastry shells, as a stuffing for
mushrooms, or with fresh asparagus
as a crepe recipe.)

MAKE-YOUR-OWN BOURSIN CHEESE

INGREDIENTS
8 oz. cream cheese, softened
2 cloves garlic, crushed
1 tsp. oregano
1/4 tsp. pepper
1/4 tsp. thyme
1/4 tsp. basil

DIRECTIONS
…Blend cream cheese, garlic,
oregano, pepper, thyme, and basil.
…Refrigerate.
…Use as a spread on crackers or
use in cooking.
…You may also use it to top steaks,
grilled chicken, and fish.

EXAMPLE IS KEY ~ Our kids are very precious to us. They are grown now and take the responsibility of their money very seriously. We started very early allowing them to manage what they earned from their allowance and chores to see how they chose to use funds. I think flexibility is the key. What works with one child may not with another. I am married to a CPA who has always said that parental example is the key. If mom and dad have good money habits, the chances are the kids will too. Think of how many ways you are similar to your own parents in how you handle your money. A good financial background is one of the most important things we can give our children. JULIE DOUTHETT

MEXICAN CHILI DIP

INGREDIENTS
Two 4 oz. cans peeled and
  chopped chilies, drained
16 oz. grated cheddar cheese
2 eggs
2 Tbsp. milk

DIRECTIONS
…Put chilies in a pie pan.
…Sprinkle cheese over the top.
…Beat eggs and milk together.
…Pour over chilies and cheese.
…Bake at 350 degrees for 25 minutes.
…Serve with crackers.

MEXICAN DIP

INGREDIENTS
3 avocados, chopped
1/2 c. sour cream
1/4 c. mayonnaise
1 package taco seasoning mix
4 oz. cheddar cheese, grated
4 oz. Monterey Jack cheese, grated
1 small can ripe olives, chopped
3 medium tomatoes, chopped
6 green onions, thinly sliced

DIRECTIONS
…Spread mashed avocados in bottom of a deep dish pie pan.
…Mix sour cream, mayonnaise, and taco mix, and spread over avocados.
…Layer cheeses, olives, tomatoes, and onions on top.
…Serve with veggies or tortilla chips.

ONE-ONE-ONE APPETIZER

INGREDIENTS
1 lb. lean ground beef
1 lb. sausage (regular or hot)
1 lb. Jalapeño or regular Velveeta
  cheese
1 package Pumpernickel or party
  sized Rye bread

DIRECTIONS
…Brown ground beef.
…Drain and set aside in a bowl.
…Brown sausage thoroughly.
…Drain and add to hamburger.
…Cube Velveeta in a skillet and
melt slowly.
…Add the meat mixture.
…Stir evenly and spread on
individual party bread.
…Place on cookie sheet and broil
until bubbling and toasted.

PECAN CHEESE SQUARES

INGREDIENTS
12 strips bacon
1/2 c. chopped pecans
1 c. sharp cheddar cheese,
  shredded
1 tsp. onion, grated
1/2 c. mayonnaise
Dash of salt
Party bread slices

DIRECTIONS:
…Preheat oven to 350 degrees.
…Fry bacon.
…Drain and crumble.
…Blend bacon, pecans, cheese,
onion, mayonnaise, and salt.
…Spread mixture on bread slices.
…Place on cookie sheet and bake
in oven until lightly browned.
(Topping may be made ahead.)

PRAIRIE FIRE CHILI DIP

INGREDIENTS
1 can (no-beans) chili
One 8 oz. package cream cheese
One 4 oz. can chopped green chilies
One 4 oz. can chopped ripe olives

DIRECTIONS
…Chop cream cheese into chunks.
…Place cheese, chili, green chilies,
and olives in a saucepan over
medium heat.
…Serve hot with corn chips.

M.I. (MILITARY INTELLIGENCE)-MOM ~ It is imperative that at all ages of development your children think that you have been thoroughly trained in espionage techniques; that your insights and powers of observation are omnipotent. They should understand that your skills also extend to their friends; that you have an uncanny sense regarding what they are thinking and planning. Simply put, trust is a commodity that is newly earned each day. It is Mom's responsibility to ascertain that honesty and trust are securely in place. Vigilance prevents many problems from developing. As Ronald Reagan liked to say, "Trust but verify."

SUSAN HORAN GARLINGHOUSE

RELUCTANT READERS ~ I have learned a few effective techniques for helping reluctant children learn the joys of reading. At bedtime, my children only had permission to keep the light on if they were reading. I'd dangle out books but pull them back saying, "This book may be too mature for you; it has some suggestive situations. I don't know if you are ready for this book!" And I would leave magazines opened to interesting articles at the breakfast counter where they ate.

SUSAN HORAN GARLINGHOUSE

ROUND-UP
CHIP BEEF DIP

INGREDIENTS
Two 8 oz. packages softened
  cream cheese
4 Tbsp. milk
5 oz. dried beef, chopped
4 Tbsp. green pepper, finely
  chopped
4 Tbsp. instant minced onion
1 c. sour cream

DIRECTIONS
…Soften onion with a small
amount of warm water.
…Mix all ingredients and pour
into greased baking dish.
…Bake at 350 degrees for 20
minutes.
…Serve hot with crackers.

SALMON MOUSSE

INGREDIENTS
1 envelope unflavored
  gelatin
1/4 c. cold water
1/2 c. boiling water
1/2 c. mayonnaise
1 Tbsp. lemon juice
1 Tbsp. grated onion
2 Tbsp. dill
1 tsp. salt
1 can salmon
1 c. heavy cream
1/4 tsp. paprika

DIRECTIONS
…Soften gelatin in cold water
in a bowl.
…Stir in boiling water until
gelatin dissolves.
…Set aside to cool.
…Stir in mayonnaise and
seasonings.
…Blend completely.
…Refrigerate 15 minutes until
mixture begins to thicken.
…Fold in salmon.
…Whip cream.
…Fold in.
…Pour into mold (fish shaped
is the most elegant) and chill
4 hours.
…Remove from mold onto
tray and serve this delicate
treat with crackers.

SEAFOOD SPREAD

INGREDIENTS

1 Tbsp. butter
2 stalks celery, chopped
1/2 green pepper, chopped
1 Tbsp. Worcestershire sauce
3/4 c. mayonnaise
1 Tbsp. lemon juice
Butter
One 6 1/2 oz. can shrimp
One 6 1/2 oz. can crabmeat
6 saltines, crushed
1/4 c. Parmesan cheese, grated

DIRECTIONS

…Sauté celery, green pepper, and Worcestershire sauce in butter until tender.
…Add mayonnaise.
…Pour lemon juice over shrimp and flaked crabmeat and add to other ingredients.
…Spoon into greased casserole dish.
…Top with saltines and then cheese.
…Dot with butter.
…Bake at 350 degrees for 20 minutes.

FAITH ~ My husband and I have felt that it is important to bring God's daily blessing to the attention of our children. So, we have planted a small herb and vegetable garden together every summer since they were babies. What great life lessons there are to be learned in nature and in the garden! We observe the varying conditions and the work needed to maintain the garden, tying it to life's reality, "every action has consequences." If you tend to the needs of the garden, it will flourish with abundance. So will a person's spirit if faithful, kind, and giving. While teaching our children to cook (my son is the most interested), they will go out to the garden and gather fresh herbs to add to the meal. It is wonderful to share time in the kitchen together! While cooking together, our conversations are always so interesting, revealing, and full of wonder. On the chalkboard next to the dinner table we write scripture passages. As we eat dinner, we chat about what these passages mean to each of us. When my husband and I were newly married, he once teased me after watching me working every night to provide a well balanced, nutritious, and unique meal, "Every meal doesn't have to be a religious experience!" He was trying to give me a break. Still, I can't think of a better way to have a "religious experience" than cooking and sharing a meal with my family. DEANA BEARDMORE

A UNIFIED FRONT ~ Kids are exceptionally skilled at exploiting differences between mom and dad. They are quick to spot unexpressed disagreements. Their skill at splitting succeeds because many parents fail to check with the other to see what was said or promised, or make insufficient efforts to reach a consensus. Many parents fail to recognize how important it is that they be "on the same page." When they are not, they are vulnerable to splitting as the children successfully play one parent against the other. The consequence: domestic chaos as each parent reacts by blaming the other, and the children run free. The problem: both parents are blind to the real issue — their failure to stick together. This makes it easy (and inevitable) that their children will exploit their differences, with all kinds of unwelcome consequences. BEV MENNINGER

PIECE OF THE PIE ~ I have two boys. Having grown up with sisters, it took me awhile to adjust to the noise level boys generate. There always seemed to be a battle of "mine." One afternoon while looking for a treat, they began arguing about sharing the last piece of cake. I remembered a technique my dad had used on me. After much arguing, I turned to my younger son who absolutely loved sweets and said, "Scott, why don't you slice the cake so you and Kevin may share it." He was delighted to have that advantage. Rather than cut the cake equally, he sliced a very large piece thinking it would be his, while leaving a meager slice for his brother. I then turned to my older son and said, "Kevin, since Scott sliced the cake, you may choose the first piece." Kevin naturally took the larger of the two pieces without a second glance at his brother. Scott began to protest until he realized he was responsible for cutting his own "piece of the pie." NANCY ALEXANDER

SEAFOOD WRAPS

INGREDIENTS

1/2 lb. salad shrimp
3/4 c. ranch dressing
1 head romaine lettuce
1/2 c. chopped celery
1 tomato, chopped
2 tsp. dill
1/2 red onion, finely chopped
3 tortillas

DIRECTIONS

…Warm tortillas for 10 seconds in the microwave.
…Paint tortilla with ranch dressing.
…Layer on lettuce, celery, tomato, dill, onion, and shrimp.
…Roll tightly and slice in half, or smaller for hors d'oeuvres.
…Arrange on a platter.

SIMPLE STUFFED MUSHROOMS

INGREDIENTS

1/2 lb. mushrooms, cleaned
8 oz. cream cheese, softened
10 slices bacon, cooked and
    crumbled

DIRECTIONS

…Mix bacon and cream cheese.
…Stuff mushrooms with mixture.
…Bake at 300 degrees for 10 minutes.
…Finish under broiler until lightly browned.

SMOKED SALMON SPREAD

INGREDIENTS

8 oz. cream cheese, softened
1/4 c. heavy cream
2 scallions, sliced
1 tsp. lemon juice
4 oz. smoked salmon, shredded
1 lemon

DIRECTIONS

…Mix cream cheese and cream.
…Stir in scallions and lemon juice.
…Gently fold in salmon.
…Spoon into a serving dish and garnish with lemon wedges.
…Serve with sturdy crackers.

SMOKIN' HOT PARTY BALLS

INGREDIENTS

One 10 oz. package sharp cheddar cheese
One 12 oz. package hot sausage
3 c. Bisquick

DIRECTIONS

…Melt cheese.
…Break up uncooked sausage with a fork and add to cooled cheese.
…Add Bisquick.
…Mix well with hands.
…Shape into walnut-sized balls.
…Bake on a cookie sheet for 20 minutes at 350 degrees.
…Roll balls around twice to brown them on all sides.
Makes 50 balls.
(Can be prepared ahead and frozen.)

SOUTHWEST TURKEY WRAP

INGREDIENTS

3 oz. sun-dried tomato cream cheese
1 tomato tortilla
3 slices smoked turkey
3 leaves romaine lettuce
1 Tbsp. chopped cilantro
Sliced red and green bell peppers
1/2 avocado, sliced
5 slices tomato

DIRECTIONS

…Warm tortilla in microwave for 10 seconds.
…Spread evenly with sun-dried tomato cream cheese.
…Layer with romaine, cilantro, peppers, turkey, tomatoes, and avocado slices.
…Wrap tightly, folding the ends.
…Serve immediately.

SPINACH BALLS

INGREDIENTS

Two 10 oz. packages frozen spinach, defrosted and squeezed dry
2 c. stuffing mix
1 c. Parmesan cheese
1/2 c. butter, melted
4 scallions, chopped
3 eggs, beaten

Sauce:
1/2 c. dry mustard
1/2 c. white wine
1/4 c. honey

DIRECTIONS

…Mix all ingredients for spinach balls and form into 1 inch balls.
…Refrigerate for one hour. (Balls may be frozen for later use.)
…Prepare sauce by mixing all ingredients and refrigerate for several hours.
…Bake balls (at room temperature) for 10 minutes at 350 degrees.
…Serve with toothpicks and sauce while balls are hot.

SUPER SIMPLE SPREAD

INGREDIENTS

3 oz. cream cheese
1 c. butter
1/4 c. Parmesan cheese
1 package ranch dressing mix
Cracked pepper

DIRECTIONS

…Mix softened cream cheese, butter, Parmesan cheese, and ranch dressing mix.
…Spread on serving dish.
…Sprinkle with cracked pepper.
…Serve with large stick pretzels.

CREATE YOUR OWN VILLAGE TO HELP RAISE YOUR CHILD ~

I think mothers should expose our children to adults from varied experiences, backgrounds, and perspectives. In that way, our children have the opportunity to grow beyond us and to become more than we are. Just standing on our shoulders is not enough.

Seek out the most interesting people you can find and make sure your child has the opportunity to experience them on whatever level is available. Sometimes the other mother has a perspective that can change lives. A good friend of mine knew to wish for things for our daughter that we didn't know existed. And she knew how to make them happen. She had an idea for a life-changing philanthropic project for our daughter to undertake (a library for a battered women's center). Our teenage daughter liked the idea more because it came from a mother other than me. She also offered for her son, who was home from college, to give advice to our daughter about her college choices, essay subject, and interview pointers when she was a senior applying for herself. In part, as a result of all this help, she was accepted to Stanford. HELEN CROW

SWISS CHEESE SPREAD

INGREDIENTS
1/2 c. mayonnaise
3 c. shredded Swiss cheese
1/2 small onion, finely chopped
Salt and pepper to taste

DIRECTIONS
…Combine mayonnaise, cheese, onion, and seasonings.
…Bake at 350 degrees until hot in center.
(Do not use microwave.)
…Serve with sturdy crackers while piping hot.

THREE ALARM SPICY SALSA

INGREDIENTS
One 14 oz. can stewed tomatoes, undrained or 3 medium tomatoes, chopped fine
6 scallions, chopped
One 4 oz. can chopped green chilies, undrained
1 small jar jalapeño peppers, seeded and minced

DIRECTIONS
…Chop tomatoes.
…Add scallions, chilies, and peppers.
…Serve with tortilla chips.

TORTILLA BEEF ROLL-UPS

INGREDIENTS
Four 12 oz. flour tortillas
One 8 oz. carton bacon horseradish dip
10 to 12 oz. thickly sliced cooked beef
Leaf Lettuce

DIRECTIONS
…Spread one side of each tortilla with 2 Tbsp. of the dip, covering the entire tortilla.
…Top with one or two slices of beef.
…Spread with another 2 Tbsp. of the dip.
…Top with lettuce leaves.
…Roll the tortilla up jelly roll style.
…Place seam side down on a platter.
…Cover and chill.
…Before serving, cut each roll-up crosswise into thirds.
(Slivered ham with horseradish mustard may also be used.)

YOU LOVE HER MORE THAN YOU LOVE ME ~

I know you cannot understand until you're a parent – you can never love one more. JANA BARRY

WISCONSIN GLAZED BRIE

INGREDIENTS
2 lb. Brie
2 c. chopped pecans
2 c. brown sugar
1/4 c. Cognac

DIRECTIONS
…Shave rind off Brie, top only.
…Place cheese in casserole serving dish.
…Cover with pecans.
…Pack brown sugar on top.
…Drizzle with Cognac.
…Bake at 300 degrees for 10 minutes.
…Serve hot with assorted crackers.

CURFEW ALARM ~ When our daughter was old enough to be out later than the time of night we wanted to go to bed, we set the alarm clock outside of our bedroom door for the time of her curfew. She knew she had better get home in time to turn that alarm off. This method worked like a charm! SHARON WIECK

TALKING TO YOUR CHILD ~ When you really want to know what's going on in your child's life, take him or her for a long drive. Let your child pick the music and then start a conversation. Often, I will start with the music itself. Why do they like it? What is the song really saying? Do their friends like it? How are things going with their friends? Before they know it, we get to what is bothering them. INES GILBERT

38/ Soups & stews

Soups & stews

LONG TRIPS? STUFF AND SNACKS ~ Traveling with your children is always a challenge, but it can be made less difficult if you remember to bring plenty of "stuff." Whether in a car or on a plane, it is critical to have enough entertainment and food for fifteen-minute increments. Books, tapes, drawing materials, and favorite toys need to be handed out one by one, not all at once, and mixed with heavy doses of snacks, gum, and drinks. (Just make certain bathrooms are available for frequent juice stops.) You may feel like a Sherpa, but plenty of stuff and snacks makes any trip bearable.

Governor of Kansas KATHLEEN SEBELIUS

ARTICHOKE AND SAUSAGE SOUP

INGREDIENTS
16 oz. sausage, mild or hot
Two cans artichoke hearts, drained
2 cans diced tomatoes
1 package onion soup mix
3 c. water
1/2 tsp. Italian seasoning

DIRECTIONS
…Crumble sausage and brown in soup pot.
…Drain grease.
…Cut artichokes into bite size pieces.
…Add to sausage.
…Add tomatoes, soup mix, water, and Italian seasoning.
…Bring to a boil and simmer one hour.
(Soup is best if made several days in advance and refrigerated.)
Serves 8 to 10.

ASPARAGUS CRAB CHOWDER

INGREDIENTS

Two 10 oz. cans cream of
  asparagus soup
3/4 c. milk
1/4 c. sherry
1 c. cream
7 1/2 oz. crabmeat
Croutons
1/4 c. fresh chopped parsley

DIRECTIONS

…Combine first five ingredients
and heat.
…Top with croutons and fresh
chopped parsley.
Serves 6.

CHICKEN CON QUESO SOUP

INGREDIENTS

1 lb. skinless chicken, cut into
  3/4 inch pieces
1 large onion, chopped
1 large green pepper, chopped
1 large red pepper, chopped
1 Tbsp. oil
1 Tbsp. chili powder
2 tsp. cumin
2 cans (15 oz.) kidney beans,
  rinsed and drained
1 can (23 oz.) whole tomatoes,
  chopped
8 oz. Velveeta
1 1/2 c. picante sauce
Fresh cilantro

DIRECTIONS

…In a Dutch oven cook chicken,
onion, and peppers in oil until chicken
is cooked.
…Add chili powder and cumin and
cook for 1 minute.
…Add beans, tomatoes, and picante
sauce and mix well.
…Bring to a boil, then reduce and
simmer for 20 minutes.
(At this point soup can be frozen or
refrigerated for later use.)
…Add Velveeta and stir until cheese is
melted and well blended.
…Garnish with chopped fresh cilantro,
avocado, and sour cream.
Makes 10 cups.

CHUCK WAGON BEEF STEW

INGREDIENTS
2 lb. cubed stew meat
2 cans diced tomatoes
One 10 oz. package baby lima beans
1 medium onion, chopped
1 large carrot, peeled and sliced
Salt and pepper
Water
1/2 c. converted rice

DIRECTIONS
…Combine meat and tomatoes with juice in a Dutch oven.
…Bake covered in a 300 degree oven for 6 to 8 hours.
…After 4 to 6 hours, stir in lima beans, onion, carrot, salt and pepper to taste, rice, and 1 c. water.
…Cover and cook another 2 hours.
…More water may need to be added toward the end of cooking time.
…Adjust seasoning.
Serves 8.

CINCINNATI CHILI

INGREDIENTS
2 lb. ground beef
1 medium onion
1 jar or can (26 oz.) chunky spaghetti sauce
1 Tbsp. chili powder
1 Tbsp. cumin
1/2 jar or can (13 oz.) water
1 can chili beans
8 oz. spaghetti pasta

DIRECTIONS
…Brown meat and onion.
…Drain.
…Add all other ingredients except spaghetti.
…Simmer.
…Cook spaghetti according to package directions.
…Place serving of spaghetti in a large soup bowl.
…Add a cup of chili.
…Top with cheddar cheese, onions, or other toppings.
Serves 6 to 8.

COLD MELON SOUP

INGREDIENTS
3 c. chopped cantaloupe (1 melon)
3 c. chopped honeydew melon (1 melon)
2 c. fresh orange juice
3 tsp. honey

DIRECTIONS
…Puree one-half of mixture for one minute and finely chop the other half.
…Blend orange juice and honey into the pureed melon.
…Serve well chilled.
(May be made the day before.)
(Champagne, mint sprig, or fresh violet blossoms may be added for garnish.)
Serves 8.

COUNTRY CHUNKY CORN CHOWDER

INGREDIENTS
6 slices bacon
2 tsp. butter
3/4 c. chopped onion
3/4 c. chopped celery
4 c. chicken stock
2 c. diced potatoes
6 c. fresh corn or three 10 oz. packages frozen
   corn, thawed
1 c. heavy cream
Salt and pepper to taste

DIRECTIONS
…Fry bacon until crisp and remove from pan.
…Add butter and melt with bacon drippings.
…Add onions and celery and cook until tender.
…Pour stock into soup pot and add potatoes.
…Cook until tender.
…Puree one 10 oz. package of corn in a blender,
adding small amount of hot stock while blending.
…Add blended corn, remaining corn,
vegetables and cream to soup pot.
…Season and heat.
…Add crumbled bacon just before serving.

A LITTLE ADVICE ~ I have no great words of wisdom for raising children other than to treat them as you would wish to be treated: with patience, understanding, honesty, and, above all, with unconditional love. Rules and expectations should be appropriate for their age, and discipline should reflect the type and severity of the infraction and their age and ability to comprehend. I think it is better to be too strict than too lenient, but a mother can also be too inflexible. It also helps to recognize the humor in situations. We can never tell our children (or our husbands, for that matter) too often that we love them. BARB RIESSEN

CRAB BISQUE

INGREDIENTS

One 10 1/2 oz. can cream of mushroom
* soup*
One 10 1/2 oz. can cream of asparagus
* soup*
1/2 soup can milk
1 c. light cream
One 7 1/2 oz. can crabmeat, flaked and
* cartilage removed*
1/4 c. dry white wine

DIRECTIONS

…Blend soups.
…Stir in milk and cream.
…Heat just to boiling.
…Add crabmeat and heat thoroughly.
…Stir in wine just before serving.
Serves 6 to 8.
(May be frozen.)

CREAM OF BRIE SOUP

INGREDIENTS

1/2 c. chopped onion
1/2 c. sliced celery
1/4 c. butter
1/4 c. flour
2 c. milk
2 c. chicken stock
3/4 lb. Brie cheese,
* rind removed*
Salt and pepper
Chives

DIRECTIONS

…In a heavy pot sauté
onion and celery in butter
until transparent.
…Stir in flour and cook
until mixture bubbles.
…Remove from heat.
…Gradually add milk and
chicken stock.
…Cube cheese.
…Add to pot and stir
until the cheese is melted.
…Season with salt and
pepper.
…Garnish with chives.
Serves 6 to 8.

CUCUMBER AVOCADO SOUP

INGREDIENTS
1 cucumber, peeled, seeded, and chopped
1 large avocado, peeled and seeded
2 scallions chopped
1 c. chicken stock
1 c. sour cream
3 tsp. lime juice
Salt to taste

DIRECTIONS
…Place all ingredients in a food processor or blender.
…Blend until smooth.
…Chill.

OOPS I DID IT AGAIN ~

When I first became a mother I wanted so much to be perfect, to set a good example, that I was afraid to admit I had made a mistake in front of my children. But I realized the best example is to admit a mistake, take responsibility, and try to rectify it. Then when my children made mistakes, they had my example of how to handle it. Instead of making excuses for them, which is often very tempting, I helped them face their mistake and accept the consequences. Then we could discuss how best for them to make amends. MARE CZYZEWSKI-ROCKEFELLER PH.D.

NICE MAY NOT BE SO NICE ~

We were too nice as parents. Someone has to be the heavy. We were like so many parents we knew — well intentioned and conscientious, but failing to stand up to our children. Knowing where they are going, who they're with and holding them accountable for schoolwork, chores, and monthly budgets is a hard and lonely job at times. They would say, "None of our friends have a curfew!" The most difficult job in parenting is striking the right balance between "toughness" and "love." MARY POWELL YORKE

DUST BOWL WHITE CHILI

INGREDIENTS

2 cans (15 oz.) white corn
2 cans (15 oz.) Great Northern beans
2 cans (4 oz.) diced green chili peppers
1 can (14 oz.) chicken broth
1 c. onion, chopped
1 Tbsp. lemon juice
1 tsp. cumin
1 clove garlic, minced
1 tsp. lemon pepper seasoning
2 c. chicken, cooked and chopped
Crushed tortilla chips
Grated cheddar or Monterey Jack cheese

DIRECTIONS

…Combine all ingredients except chicken, chips, and cheese.
…Simmer uncovered for 10 minutes.
…Stir in chicken and heat thoroughly.
…To serve, top with crushed chips and shredded cheese.
Serves 8.

ENGLISH CHEDDAR CHOWDER

INGREDIENTS

2 c. water, salted
1/2 c. carrots, finely chopped
1/2 c. celery, finely chopped
1/2 c. scallions, finely chopped
1 onion, finely chopped
1/2 c. butter
3/4 c. flour
4 c. milk, heated to boiling
4 c. chicken broth, heated to boiling
1 lb. sharp cheddar cheese, grated
1 Tbsp. mustard
Salt, pepper, and cayenne pepper to taste

DIRECTIONS

…Boil carrots, celery, and scallions in salted water for 5 minutes.
…Set aside.
…Cook onion in butter for 1 minute or until limp.
…Blend in flour.
…Slowly add hot milk and broth.
…Cook and stir with a whisk until blended and smooth.
…Add cheese, vegetables, and seasonings.
…Cook and whisk constantly until cheese is melted and soup is well blended.
Serves 8.

FRENCH ESCARGOT SOUP

INGREDIENTS
24 snails
1 clove garlic, minced
2 Tbsp. butter
3 c. beef broth
2 Tbsp. parsley
1/4 tsp. dried oregano
1/8 tsp. lemon pepper
Four 3/4 inch thick slices of French
  bread, toasted
Four 1 1/2 oz. slices of provolone cheese

DIRECTIONS
…Sauté escargot and garlic in butter
for one minute.
…Remove escargot with slotted spoon
and divide into 4 soup crocks.
…Add broth and spices to saucepan
and bring to a boil.
…Divide into the soup crocks.
…Top with bread, then cheese.
…Place crocks in preheated 375 degree
oven until cheese bubbles.
Serves 4.
(Expensive soup, but elegant.)

GAZPACHO

INGREDIENTS
2 3/4 c. celery, coarsely chopped
2/3 c. cucumber, unpeeled and
  diced
2 1/2 lb. tomatoes, seeded and
  diced
3/4 to 1 oz. canned chili pepper,
  finely diced
5 1/2 oz. tomato paste
1/4 c. onion, diced
2 Tbsp. parsley, chopped
46 oz. tomato juice

DIRECTIONS
…Combine all ingredients and
chill.
…Each bowl is garnished with a
cucumber, lemon wheel on its rim
and a black olive.
…Ingredients may be varied
according to taste and texture
desired.
(Wonderful way to use vegetables
in your garden.)
Serves 8.

HE-MAN'S ELEPHANT STEW

INGREDIENTS
1 elephant
Brown gravy
Salt and pepper to taste
2 rabbits (optional)

DIRECTIONS
…Cut elephant into bite-sized
pieces.
…This will take about 4 months.
…Cook over outdoor fire until
tender.
…Allow 6 months.
…Add salt and pepper and cover
with gravy.
…This will serve about 4,000 or
one small Midwestern town.
…If more are expected, add the
rabbits (Do this only if absolutely
necessary since most people
don't like to find a hare in
their stew.)

ALLOWANCE ~ We have a strategy designed to help our children appreciate the value of money and charity. We give them a monthly allowance, which increases slightly each year. Each child has three jars in the cupboard and when they receive their allowance they are to divide it three ways: one-third goes into the "spend" jar; one-third into the "save" jar; and one-third into the "charities" jar. Once they have a fair amount collected in the "save" jar, we go to the bank and deposit it into their savings accounts. Of course, they get to choose what causes to support with the money accumulated in the jar for charities. How you choose to divvy up the money is not as important as establishing the concept of enjoying your hard-earned cash, while still saving for a rainy day and sharing your good fortune with others. KRISTIN CHANAY

LISTEN WITHOUT JUDGMENT ~ I believe it is very important to be a good listener to your child. It is so easy to be too busy and distracted to give your attention to your child. They need to know you care about their thoughts and lives and through this you can guide, direct, and know your child. I never punished our daughter as a result of information she shared because I knew she would no longer feel safe and secure to share with me. For example, when she was in the third grade she came home from school and informed me as soon as she walked in the door that the teacher had made her mad. She then made a very disrespectful comment to the teacher, which resulted in a punishment. I asked her if she had apologized and she had, so there was no need, I felt, for us to punish her again. SHARON WIECK

HOMESTYLE CHEDDAR CHOWDER

INGREDIENTS

2 c. boiling water
2 c. diced potatoes
1/2 c. sliced carrots
1/2 c. sliced celery
1/4 c. chopped onion
1 1/2 tsp. salt
1 c. diced ham, optional
1/4 c. butter
1/4 c. flour
2 c. milk
2 c. shredded cheddar cheese
1/4 tsp. pepper

DIRECTIONS

…Cook potatoes, carrots, celery, and onion 10 to 12 minutes in water with salt.
…Do not drain.
…Melt butter, add flour, stir in milk to make white sauce.
…Add the cheese and stir until melted.
…Add the ham and vegetables.
(Do not use low-fat cheese in this recipe. Recipe may be doubled.)
Serves 8.

KANSAS CITY STEAK SOUP

INGREDIENTS

1 c. butter
1 c. flour
1/2 gal. water
2 lbs. ground beef
1 c. onion, chopped
1 c. carrots, sliced
1 c. celery, chopped
2 c. frozen mixed vegetables
2 Tbsp. beef bouillon
Salt and pepper
1 can tomatoes

DIRECTIONS

…Melt butter and stir in flour.
…Add water.
…Brown and drain beef. Add to water.
…Add all other ingredients and simmer until vegetables are tender.
(Can be frozen.)
Serves 8.

LEAH'S PUMPKIN SOUP

INGREDIENTS

15 oz. can pumpkin
1/4 c. butter
1 small onion, chopped
1/4 tsp. ginger
1/4 tsp. nutmeg
2 c. chicken broth
1 oz. brandy
1 c. cream or half and half

DIRECTIONS

…Melt butter.
…Sauté onion.
…Add ginger, nutmeg, chicken broth, and pumpkin.
…Bring to a boil.
…Lower heat and add cream.
…At the last minute add brandy.
Serves 6 to 8.
(This can be served in mini-pumpkins for very special individual servings.)

CAR OWNERSHIP ~

Our children — three girls and one boy — worked in order to buy half of a car. By sixteen, they all had cars. BUT we kept 51% ownership in case we needed to take back the keys if problems arose. Fortunately, we did not have to enforce this.

Most insurance companies give discounts for students with good grades. We gave this money to our son as a reward for strong school work. This discount carries over when a student is still in graduate school and on his or her own policy. So the savings can be very significant to a family over a lifetime. MARY ALICE MCRAE

MINNETONKA TOMATO AND WILD RICE SOUP

INGREDIENTS
1 Tbsp. butter
1 Tbsp. olive oil
1 medium onion, finely chopped
2 medium carrots, finely chopped
3 stalks celery, finely chopped
One 32 oz. can diced, peeled
  tomatoes with juice
1/2 c. tomato puree
2 c. vegetable or chicken
  broth
1/2 c. wild rice
Pepper
2 bay leaves
2 tsp. fresh basil
Cream (optional)

DIRECTIONS
…Sauté onion, carrots, and celery in butter and olive oil for 10 minutes.
…Add tomatoes, stock, bay leaves, and wild rice.
…Boil just above a simmer until rice fluffs, approximately one hour. (You may need to add some water at this point.)
…Add pepper and basil before serving.
(To indulge, add small amount of cream.)
Serves 8.

NOLAN IRISH STEW

INGREDIENTS
1/4 c. olive oil
2 lbs. stew beef, cut into 1 inch
  pieces
6 lg. garlic cloves, minced
8 c. beef stock or canned broth
2 Tbsp. tomato paste
1 Tbsp. sugar
1 Tbsp. dried thyme
1 Tbsp. Worcestershire sauce
2 bay leaves
2 Tbsp. (1/4 stick) butter
3 lb. potatoes, peeled, cut into 1/2
  inch pieces (about 7 cups)
1 lg. onion, chopped
2 c. 1/2 inch pieces peeled carrots
2 Tbsp. chopped fresh parsley

DIRECTIONS
…Heat oil in heavy, large soup pot
over medium-high heat. Add beef
and sauté until brown on all sides,
about 5 minutes. Add garlic, and
sauté 1 minute.
…Add beef stock, tomato paste,
sugar, thyme, Worcestershire sauce
and bay leaves.
…Stir to combine.
…Bring mixture to boil.
…Reduce heat to medium low
then cover and simmer for 1 hour,
stirring occasionally.
…Melt butter in another large pot
over medium heat.
…Add potatoes, onion, and carrots.
…Sauté vegetables until golden,
about 20 minutes.
…Add vegetables to beef stew.
…Simmer uncovered until
vegetables and beef are very tender,
about 40 minutes.
…Discard bay leaves.
…Tilt pan and spoon off fat.
…Transfer to serving bowl.
…Sprinkle with parsley and serve.
Serves 10 to 12.

MULLIGAN STEW

INGREDIENTS
3 lbs. beef stew, cut into 1 1/2 inch
  cubes
6 potatoes, peeled and chopped
6 to 8 medium onions, chopped
2 c. carrots, peeled and sliced
1 c. celery, chopped
1 can tomatoes
1 Tbsp. sugar
1/2 tsp. pepper
1 tsp. garlic salt
2 tsp. salt

DIRECTIONS
…Combine all ingredients.
…Bake covered at 250 degrees for 5
hours.
…Stir occasionally.
Serves 8 to 10.

PARTY BROTH

INGREDIENTS
1 can beef broth
10 oz. tomato juice
10 oz. clam juice
1 lemon, thinly sliced

DIRECTIONS
…Combine beef broth and
tomato and clam juices.
…Simmer 10 minutes.
…Serve with a lemon slice
on top.
Serves 4.

SPICY APPLE BLOSSOM SOUP

INGREDIENTS
1 can (10 3/4 oz.) condensed
    tomato soup
1/2 soup can apple cider
1/2 soup can water
Cinnamon
Lemon slices

DIRECTIONS
…Combine soup, cider, and water
in a saucepan over medium heat.
…Heat and stir occasionally.
…Garnish with a sprinkle of
cinnamon and lemon slices.
Makes 2 servings.

TACO SOUP

INGREDIENTS
1 lb. ground chuck
1 large onion, chopped
3 cans (15 1/4 oz.) Mexican style
    chili beans
1 can (15 1/4 oz.) whole kernel corn
1 can (14 1/2 oz.) diced tomatoes
1 can (4 1/2 oz.) chopped green
    chilies
1 envelope taco seasoning mix
3 qts. water

DIRECTIONS
…Cook beef and onions until meat
is browned and onions tender.
…Drain.
…Add all other ingredients.
…Do not drain.
…Simmer uncovered for 15 minutes.
…Stir occasionally.
…Spoon into bowls.
…Top with desired toppings (i.e.
corn chips, sour cream, or cheddar
cheese.)

TWO-ALARM CHILI

INGREDIENTS
2 lb. ground beef
One 16 oz. can tomatoes
1 can water
1 can beer
1 large onion, chopped
4 cloves garlic, minced
1 Tbsp. chili powder
1 Tbsp. cumin

DIRECTIONS
…Sear meat until brown. Drain.
…Chop tomatoes until chunky.
…Add to meat along with
liquids, onion and garlic.
…Simmer for one hour.
…Stir occasionally.
(Add hot sauce or chili powder
to set mouths afire.)
Serves 6 to 8.

ZUCCHINI SOUP

INGREDIENTS
4 zucchini, quartered and sliced
Two 15 oz. cans chicken broth
1 bunch green onions
1 tsp. salt
1 tsp. pepper
Dill weed to taste
Two 8 oz. packages cream cheese
1 c. sour cream with chives

DIRECTIONS
…Boil all ingredients except
cheeses for 20 minutes.
…Place in blender.
…Add cream cheese and sour
cream with chives.
…Blend until smooth.
…Serve hot or cold.
…Garnish with chives.
(May be frozen.)
Serves 10.

TEACHING TOLERANCE ~ We wanted our children to learn an appreciation and tolerance of diverse cultures. We found the best way to do this was to host foreign exchange students in our home over the school years. Students from England, Guatemala, Brazil and Italy provided our children with the opportunity to learn new languages, customs, and cultures unlike our own. This gave them a taste for international travel so when they were old enough, they became exchange students themselves. Their travels were an education that cannot be measured in dollars and cents. CINDY GIESSEL

54 / Salads & dressings

Salads & dressings

BABY GREENS WITH VINAIGRETTE AND SPICED ALMONDS

INGREDIENTS

5 large handfuls of baby greens
Spiced almonds (see page 67)
4 fresh plums cut into wedges
  and seeded
Plum vinaigrette (see page 71)

DIRECTIONS

…Arrange baby greens on a salad plate.
…Ladle desired amount of dressing on salad and garnish with plums and almonds.
Serves 5.

BLUE CHEESE POTATO SALAD

INGREDIENTS

4 large potatoes, peeled and cubed
1/2 c. chopped celery
1/2 c. chopped scallions
3 Tbsp. minced parsley
1/2 Tbsp. celery seed
1 c. sour cream
2 to 4 oz. blue cheese, crumbled
3 Tbsp. white wine vinegar

DIRECTIONS

…Boil potatoes until tender. Drain.
…Combine celery, scallions, parsley, salt, pepper, and celery seed with potatoes.
…In a separate bowl combine sour cream, blue cheese, and vinegar.
…Pour over potato mixture and toss.
(May be made the day ahead and refrigerated.)

BROCCOLI RAISIN SALAD

INGREDIENTS

4 c. chopped fresh broccoli
1 red onion, finely chopped
3/4 c. raisins
6 slices bacon, fried crisp and
  crumbled
1/2 c. sunflower seeds

Dressing:
3/4 c. mayonnaise
1/4 c. sugar
2 Tbsp. vinegar

DIRECTIONS

…Mix all ingredients except bacon and sunflower seeds.
…Refrigerate several hours or overnight.
…Add bacon and sunflower seeds just before serving.

SENSE OF HUMOR ~

I found out early on that my default mode as a parent was to be too serious: to lecture, to be hard on myself. It is not easy negotiating ceasefires between warring siblings, cleaning toothpaste off a child's clean shirt, or discovering the item sticking on the refrigerator is not food, but, as my three-year-old once put it, the "no-no smell." But slowly I have learned that humor is the most effective way to deal with problems and maintain my sanity. I try to remember to do something deliberately silly when problems arise. I take their hat and stumble around to their cheers. Or I use a silly voice. Or put on a "magical" sweater that makes mommy dance. Or chase them around the house crying "I'm gonna get you." Or balance a small beanbag animal on their head, while asking, "What is growing in your hair?" There are so many ways to make them smile. And it always makes my day.

MARY MARTELL

CHERRY COLA SALAD

INGREDIENTS
One #2 can Bing cherries
One 3 oz. package cherry
  gelatin
1 c. cola
One 8 oz. can crushed
  pineapple
Nuts (optional)

DIRECTIONS
…Pour juice from cherries into measuring cup.
…Add water to make one cup. Heat.
…Dissolve gelatin in juice.
…Add cola, cherries, pineapple, and nuts.
…Chill until firm.

Rides Without Recriminations

Adolescence is a particularly difficult time for young people to socialize. Peer pressure is at its highest, as is a desire to experiment with high risk behaviors. I made a deal with each of my teens that if they ever found themselves in a social situation that made them uncomfortable, they could call home for an emergency "ride home." Key to the contract was my <u>not</u> asking questions or lecturing them later about the incident. Instead they would focus on the courage to know when to leave a party and stick to their values, because these are the key to maturity, regardless of age.

LINDA VANDEGARDE

CHICKEN PASTA SALAD

INGREDIENTS

8 oz. bow tie pasta, or homemade pasta
4 c. cubed, cooked chicken
4 c. snow peas
4 scallions, chopped
1/2 c. slivered almonds, toasted

Dressing:
1 c. mayonnaise
6 Tbsp. soy sauce
1/4 tsp. ginger
1/4 c. sherry
Salt and pepper

DIRECTIONS

…Cook pasta and cool.
…Mix all other salad ingredients.

For dressing: Mix mayonnaise, soy sauce, sherry, ginger, salt, and pepper. Pour over pasta and chill. (Recipe may be doubled.)
Serves 8 to 10.

CHINESE CHICKEN SALAD

INGREDIENTS

4 c. chicken, chopped and cooked
1 c. celery, chopped
1 c. green pepper, chopped
1/2 c. ripe olives, chopped
1/4 c. onion, chopped
One 20 oz. can pineapple tidbits, drained
3 Tbsp. mustard
1 package Chow Mein noodles
1 1/2 c. mayonnaise

DIRECTIONS

…Mix all ingredients except the Chow Mein noodles.
…Just before serving add noodles to mixture.
…Serve on large lettuce leaves.
Serves 8.

NEWBORN FEEDINGS - When mom is nursing or feeding a newborn, sometimes an older brother or sister can feel left out or take advantage of the fact that mom is preoccupied. I found that preparing little bags of snacks such as dried cereal, pretzels, raisins, M&M's, etc., and presenting one to the other child to eat while the baby eats helps make feeding times special for the older sibling too.

TERRY SCHWARTZ

CRUNCHY CITRUS CHICKEN SALAD

INGREDIENTS

Assorted lettuce and cabbage greens
2 lbs. cooked chicken breasts, cubed
2 packages Ramen noodles
1 stick butter
1 lb. cooked bacon, crumbled
2 bunches green onions
1 can sliced pineapple chunks, drained
1 can mandarin oranges, drained
4 oz. sliced almonds
4 oz. sunflower seeds

Dressing
2 Tbsp. soy sauce
1/2 c. tarragon vinegar
1 c. sugar
1 c. oil

DIRECTIONS

…Melt butter in skillet.
…Crumble Ramen noodles into butter and sauté until brown.
…Mix all remaining salad ingredients together in a large bowl.
…Mix dressing ingredients together.
…Pour dressing over salad 15 minutes before serving.
…Mix in noodles.
…Toss and serve with fresh rolls.
Serves 8 to 10.

EARLY COMMUNICATION SKILLS ~ Say "YES" to your children. Begin as soon as they can nod their heads. In fact, begin with baby sign language. Sign for "more," "up," "hat," etc. They get very excited at the fact that they can communicate and achieve a desired response. It serves as the stimuli to develop a very verbal child! And it is so much fun for the mother!

BETTY CLELAND

CURRIED HARVEST FRUIT

INGREDIENTS

One 12 oz. package mixed dried fruit
One 13 oz. can pineapple chunks
One 21 oz. can cherry pie filling
1/2 c. dry sherry
1/4 c. water
1 tsp. curry powder

DIRECTIONS

…Cut large pieces of dried fruit in half.
…In a two qt. casserole, combine dried fruit and undrained pineapple chunks.
…Mix pie filling, sherry, water, and curry powder.
…Pour over fruit.
…Bake at 350 degrees for 1 hour.
…Serves 8.

CURRIED TURKEY SALAD

INGREDIENTS

8 c. diced turkey
1 lb. grapes, halved
2 c. sliced celery
Two 1 lb. cans pineapple chunks
1 c. slivered almonds, toasted
Lettuce leaves

Dressing:
3 c. mayonnaise
1 Tbsp. curry
2 Tbsp. soy sauce
2 Tbsp. lemon juice

DIRECTIONS

…Mix turkey, grapes, celery, pineapple, and almonds.
…Place in bowl.
…Mix mayonnaise, curry, soy sauce, and lemon juice, and pour over chicken.
…Serve on lettuce leaves.
Serves 8 to 10.

FROZEN FRUIT SALAD/DESSERT

INGREDIENTS
1 can cherry pie filling
One 12 oz. can crushed pineapple, undrained
1/4 c. chopped fresh apple, unpeeled
One 8 oz. can fruit cocktail, drained
1 can sweetened condensed milk
One 12 oz. carton whipped topping

DIRECTIONS
…Mix all ingredients together and freeze in a 9x13 inch pan or 2 smaller pans.
Serves 16.
(This will keep for several days and may be used for a salad or dessert.)

FROZEN WALDORF SALAD

INGREDIENTS
2 eggs, slightly beaten
1/2 c. sugar
1/2 c. pineapple juice
Dash salt
1/2 c. celery, diced
1/2 c. pineapple, drained
1/2 c. chopped pecans
1 c. whipped topping

DIRECTIONS
…Put eggs, sugar, pineapple juice, and salt in a saucepan.
…Cook over low heat stirring constantly until thick.
…Cool.
…Add celery, pineapple, pecans, and whipped topping.
…Freeze in flat serving dish.
…Set out of freezer 30 minutes before serving.
Serves 8.

FRUIT FLUFF

INGREDIENTS
One 20 oz. can crushed pineapple, drained
1 can sweetened condensed milk
1 1/2 c. miniature marshmallows
1 can blueberry pie filling
One 12 oz. carton whipped topping
1 c. pecans, chopped

DIRECTIONS
…Mix all ingredients together and refrigerate.
(Serve in goblet glasses as a luncheon or dinner dessert.)
Serves 10.

LIME PINE SALAD/DESSERT

INGREDIENTS
8 oz. cream cheese
8 oz. whipped topping
8 oz. crushed pineapple
Two 3 oz. boxes lime gelatin
1 c. chopped pecans
2 c. marshmallows

DIRECTIONS
…Soften cream cheese.
…Add whipped topping,
pineapple, and gelatin (which
has been dissolved with marshmallows in 1 c. hot water.)
…Stir in nuts. Cool.
…Pour into mold and refrigerate
for 4 hours.

MADISON COUNTY HOT CHICKEN SALAD

INGREDIENTS
2 c. diced chicken, cooked
1 c. celery, chopped
1/2 c. slivered almonds
One 2 oz. jar mushroom pieces
2 Tbsp. onion, diced
2 tsp. lemon juice
1 c. mayonnaise
1/2 c. grated cheddar cheese
1 c. potato chips, crushed
1 pie crust

DIRECTIONS
…Mix chicken, celery, almonds,
mushrooms, onion, lemon juice,
and mayonnaise lightly.
…Pour into baked pie crust.
…Sprinkle with cheese and
potato chips.
…Bake at 450 degrees for 10
to 15 minutes.

MANDARIN LETTUCE SALAD

INGREDIENTS
1/2 head red lettuce
1/2 head iceberg lettuce
11 oz. can mandarin oranges,
  drained and chilled
1 medium red onion, thinly sliced
  and separated into rings
1 green bell pepper, separated
  into rings
1/2 c. walnuts (Native black
  walnuts are found along
  Kansas streams and add a
  special taste to this salad.)
Fresh mushrooms
Sliced avocado

DIRECTIONS
…Mix lettuce.
…Add oranges, onion, green
pepper, walnuts, blue cheese,
mushrooms, and avocado.
…Toss with dressing just
before serving. (Dressing
recipe on next page.)
Serves 8.

MANDARIN ORANGE LETTUCE SALAD

INGREDIENTS
Salad:
6 slices bacon, cooked and crumbled
1/4 c. toasted almonds
One 8 oz. can mandarin oranges
1 ripe avocado
Fresh mushrooms, sliced
2 large heads Bibb or Boston lettuce
Celery, chopped
Scallions, chopped

Dressing for both salads:
1/2 c. salad oil
1/4 c. apple cider vinegar
1/4 c. sugar
1/2 tsp. salt
1/4 tsp. dry mustard
1/2 tsp. celery salt
Pepper to taste

DIRECTIONS
…Combine salad ingredients.
…Combine dressing ingredients.
…Pour dressing over chilled salad and toss immediately before serving.
Serves 8.

MEXICAN SALAD

INGREDIENTS
1 head lettuce, torn into bite size pieces
1 can ranch style beans, drained
1 onion, chopped
2 tomatoes, chopped
10 oz. grated cheddar cheese
1 lb. hamburger, browned and drained
8 oz. bottled Catalina salad dressing
One 10.5 oz. bag crushed corn chips

DIRECTIONS
…Combine lettuce, beans, onions, tomatoes, cheese, and browned hamburger 30 minutes to 1 hour before serving.
…Toss with salad dressing and refrigerate.
…At serving time, add crushed corn chips and garnish with additional cheese and tomatoes.
Serves 8.

ORGANIZATIONAL SKILLS ~ I found the best way to avoid the chaos of early morning school preparation was to teach my children to prepare the night before. I had them lay out their clothes and pack their books into their backpacks before they went to sleep. It saved loads of time and avoided the need for many arguments. BETTY CLELAND

PRETZEL SALAD/DESSERT

INGREDIENTS

2 c. crushed pretzels
1 1/2 sticks margarine, melted
1/4 c. sugar
8 oz. cream cheese, softened
1 c. sugar
6 oz. box strawberry gelatin
1 1/2 c. whipped topping
One 20 oz. can crushed pineapple,
   drain and save juice
Two 10 oz. packages frozen
   strawberries, thaw, drain well,
   and save juice

DIRECTIONS

…Mix pretzels, margarine, and
sugar.
…Press into 9x13 inch casserole.
…Bake at 350 degrees for 10
minutes.
…Cool.
…Mix cream cheese and 1 c.
sugar.
…Add whipped topping.
…Spread over crust.
…Dissolve gelatin in juices and
enough water to equal 2 cups.
…Heat gelatin and refrigerate
until syrupy.
…Add pineapple and strawberries
and spread over cream cheese.
…Chill.
Serves 8 to 10.

RASPBERRY PEAR SALAD

INGREDIENTS

4 fresh pears, peeled and sliced
1/2 c. fresh raspberries
1/2 c. toasted pecans
1 head Bibb lettuce

Vinaigrette:
1/2 c. light olive oil
1/4 c. raspberry vinegar
1 tsp. sugar
1 Tbsp. Crème Fraîche

DIRECTIONS

…Prepare vinaigrette by mixing all
ingredients and chill for several hours.
…At serving time arrange pears
carefully on lettuce.
…Top with raspberries and pecans.
…Drizzle vinaigrette over the plate.
Serves 4 to 6.

KITCHEN CONTROL ~ Cooking meals is one thing. Cooking meals and keeping control of crawling babies and fighting siblings while answering homework questions is something else. Over the years, I developed several strategies for containing the chaos. First of all, I collected recipes that could be prepared ahead of time and didn't need a great deal of supervision (unlike my children!). For example, beef stew. I also tried to make the kitchen a kid-friendly area so it wasn't as necessary to chase the kids around the house. Toddler toys were kept in plastic containers in a bottom drawer away from the stove. The kitchen table doubled as a homework center so I could supervise their work while preparing dinner. And when the food was ready, the older child cleared the table and set it for dinner. Kansas State Senator ALICIA SALISBURY

NEIGHBORHOOD MOM ~ I've always believed a mother isn't just a member of a family but also a part of the neighborhood. My children are grown and gone, and they do not have their own children yet. So I find great joy in meeting the new young children that move into our neighborhood. When I was a child, my grandmother had a gum drawer. Whenever we visited we got to pick our own package. So when my children went to college, I started a candy drawer in my pantry stocked with suckers, Life Savers, and candy bars. When neighborhood kids stop to visit, they get to take a treat home, if it is okay with their mothers. I knew the drawer's fame had grown when I said to a young boy who was visiting for the first time, "I have a candy drawer just for you." The little boy looked up and said, "I know! It's over there!" LINDA POLLY

RED RASPBERRY SALAD

INGREDIENTS
One 3 oz. package raspberry gelatin
1 c. applesauce
One 10 oz. package frozen red
  raspberries
1 c. miniature marshmallows
1 c. sour cream

DIRECTIONS
…Dissolve gelatin in 1 c. boiling
water.
…Add applesauce and raspberries.
…Stir until berries are softened.
…Refrigerate in serving dish
until firm.
…Combine marshmallows with
sour cream.
…Spread on top of gelatin.
Serves 8.

SHRIMP AND APPLE SALAD

INGREDIENTS
1 c. cooked, canned or fresh
  shrimp
1 c. red apple, chopped
1/3 c. mayonnaise
Two scallions, chopped
1/8 tsp. curry powder
1 Tbsp. lemon juice
Salt and pepper to taste

DIRECTIONS
…Place all ingredients in
a bowl.
…Toss lightly.
…Chill.
(You may substitute crab or
tuna in this recipe.)
Serves 4.

SMOKED TURKEY SALAD

INGREDIENTS
1 c. wild rice
3 c. chicken stock
1 lb. smoked turkey, diced
2 avocados, peeled and chopped
1 Tbsp. lemon juice
3/4 c. diced onion
1/4 c. red wine vinegar
1/2 c. olive oil
1/4 c. chopped parsley
Salt and pepper

DIRECTIONS
…Boil wild rice in chicken stock
and simmer for 45 minutes.
…Drain and cool.
…Transfer to bowl.
…Add turkey.
…Sprinkle avocado with lemon juice.
…Add to rice.
…Add remaining ingredients.
…Toss gently.
…Chill.
Serves 6 to 8.

SPICED ALMONDS FOR LETTUCE SALADS

INGREDIENTS
1 c. blanched almonds
2 oz. vinegar
1 Tbsp. salt
Pinch of cayenne pepper
Pinch of white pepper
1/4 c. sugar

DIRECTIONS
…Preheat oven to 350 degrees.
…Combine vinegar, salt, cayenne, white pepper, and sugar in mixing bowl and let sit for 10 minutes.
…Gently toss the almonds in the marinade and place on a non-stick cookie sheet, spreading them evenly .
…Bake for approximately 5 minutes or until golden brown.
…Check and turn often.

SPINACH STRAWBERRY SALAD

INGREDIENTS
10 oz. fresh spinach
1 c. sliced celery, cut on diagonal
1 c. sugar
1 c. pecans
1/2 c. sugar
2 tsp. salt
2 tsp. dry mustard
2/3 c. vinegar
4 scallions, chopped
2 c. oil
3 Tbsp. poppy seeds
1 pint fresh sliced strawberries

DIRECTIONS
…For caramelized pecans, combine 1 c. sugar, and pecans in a heavy skillet.
…Slowly cook until pecans have sugar melted onto them and are brown.
…Place on waxed paper.
…Cool.

…For dressing, combine salt, 1/2 c. sugar, mustard, vinegar, and scallions in blender.
…Slowly add oil.
…Stir in poppy seeds.

…For salad, combine spinach, celery, halved strawberries, and pecans.
…Coat with small amount of dressing.
…Toss.
Serves 8.

THE USED CAR ~ Our son, Noel, has always been motivated and excelled in high school. His '62 Chevy truck served him well, but he was going to need another <u>used</u> car for college. Off and on during his Junior and Senior years of high school, he and his dad would window shop for cars. The spring of his Senior year he told us he had chosen the <u>new</u> car he wanted for college. "No way!" we told him in unison. "A used car for university, a new one after graduation." Our son turned into someone we didn't recognize: sullen, argumentative, depressed. After two weeks of this, we devised a plan. We told him we had changed our minds. He could have the new car now instead of waiting until graduation unlike his older sister, Joelle, had. We told him to pick the car he wanted, and we would get the insurance papers for him to sign, since he would have to pay all of this plus gas. After all, he was getting a new car early so he would have to assume all the responsibilities for it. Within the week he found a lovely <u>used</u> vehicle and told us he just couldn't afford the <u>new</u> car yet. We had our son back on track. He graduated from Kansas State on schedule but decided to wait for the <u>new</u> car until after he finished his masters in two years. He drove the same <u>used</u> car for seven years! CAROLE ETZEL

SUMMER CABBAGE SALAD

INGREDIENTS
2 packages shredded cabbage (2 lbs.)
6 green onions, diced
4 oz. slivered almonds
4 oz. sunflower seeds
3 Tbsp. sesame seeds
2 c. diced cooked chicken
2 packages Ramen noodles, broken into pieces. (Remove flavor packet.)

DIRECTIONS
…Mix all ingredients in a bowl.
…Toss with Cabbage Salad Dressing. (See page 70.)
Serves 8.

TRADITIONAL GREEK SALAD

INGREDIENTS

*Three medium fresh tomatoes, cut
  in wedges*
1 cucumber, peeled and thinly sliced
1 c. Greek olives
1/2 medium red onion, thinly sliced
1 green pepper, cut into strips
6 oz. crumbled feta cheese
1/4 c. extra virgin olive oil
3 Tbsp. red wine vinegar
*1 package All Purpose Greek
  Seasoning*
1/2 c. parsley, chopped
Kosher salt
Black pepper

DIRECTIONS

*…Combine vegetables, olives, and
parsley in salad bowl.*
*…Sprinkle crumbled feta cheese
over vegetables.*
*…Combine oil and red wine
vinegar in a small container with
lid and shake well.*
…Pour over salad.
*…Season with salt, pepper, and
Greek seasoning.*
*…Let salad marinate until ready
to serve.*
*(Serve with pita bread heated on a
hot griddle.)*

VERMOUTH FRUIT

INGREDIENTS

1 pint fresh strawberries
One 11 oz. can mandarin oranges
1 fresh pineapple, chopped
Grapes (optional)
1/2 c. extra dry vermouth
1/4 tsp. cinnamon
1/4 c. sugar

DIRECTIONS

*…Add fruit (except strawberries)
to cinnamon and sugar.*
…Stir.
…Refrigerate for one hour.
…Strain off sugar and juice.
…Pour vermouth over fruit.
*…Stir. Refrigerate one hour
before serving.*
…Can be made 3 days ahead.
*…Add the strawberries the day
of serving so they don't discolor.*
Serves 4 to 6.

DRESSINGS

BLEU CHEESE DRESSING

INGREDIENTS
1 c. sour cream
1 c. mayonnaise
1/2 tsp. dry mustard
1/2 tsp. pepper
1/2 tsp. salt
2 tsp. Worcestershire sauce
4 oz. bleu cheese, crumbled

DIRECTIONS
…Blend all ingredients except
the bleu cheese.
…Add bleu cheese and stir.
…Refrigerate several hours before
serving.
(You may add extra bleu cheese
for extra thick dressing.)
(This dressing can be used for
salads or as a topping for steak.)

CABBAGE SALAD DRESSING

INGREDIENTS
2 Tbsp. soy sauce
1 c. sugar
1 c. sunflower oil
1/2 c. tarragon vinegar
1/2 tsp. pepper
Salt to taste
1 seasoning packet from Ramen
   noodles.

DIRECTIONS
…Mix well.
…Pour over Summer Cabbage
Salad (page 68) and chill for 15
minutes.
(Provides dressing for 6 to 8
servings.)

COUNTRY BACON DRESSING

INGREDIENTS
3 Tbsp. sugar
3 Tbsp. cider vinegar
2 tsp. chopped onion
1/4 c. mayonnaise
1/4 c. sour cream
5 slices bacon, cooked crisp and
   crumbled

DIRECTIONS
…Mix sugar, vinegar, and onion.
…Stir well to dissolve sugar.
…Whisk in mayonnaise and sour
cream until smooth.
…Add bacon and stir.
(This dressing is delicious with any
type of greens.)

MANDARIN LETTUCE SALAD DRESSING

INGREDIENTS
1/3 c. oil
1/3 c. cider vinegar
2 Tbsp. sugar
1/2 tsp. basil
Garlic to taste

DIRECTIONS
…Mix, all ingredients, chill, and shake well before using.

PLUM VINAIGRETTE SALAD DRESSING

INGREDIENTS
5 red sweet plums
1/2 c. red wine or red wine vinegar
1 Tbsp. shallots, minced
2 tsp. garlic, minced
1 1/2 to 2 c. salad oil
Salt and pepper to taste
Sugar (optional)

DIRECTIONS
…Preheat oven to 325 degrees.
…Wash plums, lightly coat with oil, place in an oven safe dish and bake for 25 minutes until soft and caramelized.
…Cool.
…Combine vinegar, shallots, garlic, and plums in a processor or blender and puree.
…If mixture is too thick, add a Tbsp. of water at a time to thin.
…Slowly drizzle in the oil.
…Season with salt and pepper.
…Chill.
…If plums are very tart, add a touch of sugar to sweeten.

Bread

biscuits &

muffins

THE FARM WORK ETHIC ~ In the Midwest work ranks right up there with religion in many families. My three siblings and I were raised on a corn and soybean farm in Iowa. This meant that every scorching August our father had us "walk the bean fields" from dawn to dusk chopping the weeds by hand with a hoe. He called it "character development." When each of us was old enough to go to college, he told us, "If you fail in school, you can always come back to this. I have hoes with each of your names on them." We got the message. All my siblings went to either law or medical school.

When my children were old enough, I started them on the next generation of character building sessions. They grew up in the suburbs, not a farm. But there was still a large lawn with growing grass in the summer, many trees with leaves in need of raking in the fall, and a long driveway repeatedly covered with snow during the winter. Whenever one of my two children complained about one of their chores, I retold the "bean field" story. When they were going off to college, I told them the lawn was always waiting for them. They did very well in school, never moved back in, and now live in apartments without lawns. Every parent needs a "bean field" story. LINDA POLLY

APRICOT BANANA
NUT BREAD

INGREDIENTS
2 ripe bananas
1/2 c. butter
1 1/2 c. flour
3/4 c. sugar
2 eggs
1/4 c. milk
2 tsp. lemon juice
1 tsp. baking soda
1/2 tsp. salt
1/2 c. chopped walnuts
1 c. dried apricots, cut in small pieces

DIRECTIONS
…Beat bananas and softened butter.
…Add flour, sugar, eggs, milk, lemon juice, baking soda, and salt in that order.
…Fold in walnuts and apricots.
…Pour into greased loaf pan.
…Bake 55 to 60 minutes in a 350 degree oven.
…Cool 10 minutes and remove from pan.

APRICOT BREAD

INGREDIENTS
1 c. dried apricots
1 c. sugar
2 Tbsp. butter
1 egg
1/4 c. water
1/2 c. orange juice
2 c. flour
2 tsp. baking powder
1/4 tsp. soda
1 tsp. salt
1/2 c. nuts

DIRECTIONS
…Soak apricots in warm water that covers the fruit until they soften.
…Drain and cut apricots with scissors into 1/4 pieces.
…Mix with sugar, butter, and egg.
…Stir in water and orange juice.
…Add flour, baking powder, soda, and salt.
…Blend in nuts and apricots.
…Pour into loaf pan.
…Bake at 350 degrees for 50 to 60 minutes.
…Remove from pan and cool on rack.

BUCKEYE BALLS

INGREDIENTS
1 1/2 c. creamy peanut butter
1/2 c. butter
1 tsp. vanilla
4 c. powdered sugar
6 oz. chocolate chips
2 Tbsp. shortening

DIRECTIONS
…Mix peanut butter, butter, vanilla, and powdered sugar well.
…Roll into small balls and chill.
…Melt chocolate chips and shortening until smooth.
…Dip peanut balls into chocolate.

OUT OF THE CLOSET ~ My son is gay. It took a long time for me to be able to talk about this in our family, or even admit it to myself. This realization was even harder for my husband. But it is true. I have finally come to peace with the fact that I am not responsible. It is a fact of nature. My son has lived out of the state for a long time, so it was easier for me to hide from this fact and in the process hide him from our friends and neighbors. I deeply regret that I made it so difficult for him, since he could not talk to me about his companions or bring them home to visit. Because of this he became closer to his friends, both male and female, than me. If I could turn back time, I would sit my son down and bring up the subject myself. It didn't go away because I ignored it. He is handsome, giving, well liked, and successful in his career. And I love him very much. I regret the time and closeness I lost because of my prejudices. I watched him grow up, and now he must do the same for me. MEREDITH WILLIAMS

MUSIC ~ Music has always been a part of my life, and I still remember the melodies our family sang together when I was a child. When my children were born I began singing to them immediately. I sang every night as I rocked them to sleep, and I entered their room each day with a smile and a happy "good morning" song. They were always in a cheerful mood when they awoke. I like to think this practice helped to prepare them to be positive, happy individuals. DIANE SNEED

COOK-OFF CHEESE SQUARES

INGREDIENTS
1 lb. butter, softened
4 jars Old English Cheese
1 tsp. Tabasco
1 tsp. onion powder
1 1/2 tsp. Worcestershire sauce
Dash cayenne pepper
2 tsp. dill weed
1 1/2 tsp. Beau Monde seasoning
1 to 2 loaves white sandwich bread

DIRECTIONS
...Make a paste of all ingredients except bread.
...Trim crusts off all bread slices.
...Make 3 layers and spread mixture on the 2 inside layers.
...Cut each one into 4 squares and then frost the top and sides with the paste and freeze on a cookie sheet.
...Place in freezer bags and keep frozen until ready to serve.
...Bake at 350 degrees for 15 minutes.

COUNTRY BISCUITS

INGREDIENTS
6 c. flour
1/2 c. instant nonfat
   milk powder
1/4 c. baking powder
2 tsp. salt
1 1/2 tsp. cream of tartar
2 c. shortening
1/4 c. sugar
1 1/2 c. water

DIRECTIONS
...Mix all ingredients well except water and shortening.
...Cut shortening into flour mixture.
...Stir 1 1/2 c. water into mixture until moistened.
...Knead 8 to 10 times.
...Divide into 2 parts.
...Roll dough 3/4 inch thick.
...Cut into 2 1/2 inch rounds.
...Brush tops with melted butter.
...Freeze on cookie sheet.
...Store in plastic bags.
(These will stay frozen for up to 3 months.)
...Bake as many as you need.
...If frozen, bake at 400 degrees for 30 to 35 minutes.
...If not frozen, bake at 400 degrees for 20 to 25 minutes.

CRANBERRY NUT BREAD

INGREDIENTS
2 c. flour
1 c. sugar
1 1/2 tsp. baking powder
1 1/2 tsp. soda
1/2 tsp. salt
1 egg, beaten
Juice and zest of 1 orange
1 c. cranberries, chopped
1 c. nuts, chopped
(walnuts or pecans)

DIRECTIONS
…Preheat oven to 350 degrees.
…Grease 9x5 loaf pan.
…Stir dry ingredients and add egg.
…Juice and zest orange.
…Add boiling water to orange juice
and zest to equal 3/4 cup.
…Add to flour mixture.
…Fold in nuts and cranberries.
…Pour into pan and bake for 1 hour.
Makes 1 loaf.

GARLIC HERB BREAD

INGREDIENTS
1 large loaf French bread, split
    lengthwise
3/4 c. butter, softened
4 scallions, including tops, finely
    chopped
1 clove garlic, crushed
1/2 tsp. marjoram
1/2 tsp. oregano
One 3 oz. can ripe olives, drained
    and chopped
1/2 c. grated Parmesan cheese
Paprika

DIRECTIONS
…Combine all ingredients except
the cheese and paprika.
…Spread evenly over both sides of
the bread.
…Sprinkle tops with Parmesan
cheese and paprika.
…Bake at 350 degrees until heated.
…Broil 2 minutes.
…Slice into serving pieces.

GRAND MARNIER FRENCH TOAST

INGREDIENTS
8 slices French bread, 3/4
    inch thick
4 eggs
1 c. milk
2 Tbsp. Grand Marnier
    liqueur
1/2 tsp. vanilla
1/4 tsp. salt
1 Tbsp. sugar

DIRECTIONS
…Place bread in a 9x13
casserole dish.
…Mix milk, Grand Marnier,
sugar, vanilla, and salt.
…Pour over bread slices.
…Turn once.
…Cover.
…Refrigerate overnight.
…Fry in lightly oiled skillet.
…Dust with powdered sugar.

HARVEST SPOON BREAD

INGREDIENTS
1 c. yellow corn meal
2 c. water
1/2 tsp. salt
1/4 c. butter
4 large eggs
1 c. milk
1/2 c. cream

DIRECTIONS
…Cook corn meal in salted water
until stiff.
…Stir constantly over medium heat.
…Cool mixture in bowl while buttered
2 qt. baking dish is heating in oven at
450 degrees.
…Add butter to corn meal.
…Add cream and eggs, one at
a time.
…Add milk and beat.
…Pour batter into hot baking dish.
…Bake 25 minutes at 450 degrees.
Serves 6.

HAZEL'S BANANA MUFFINS

INGREDIENTS
1/2 c. shortening
1 c. sugar
1 egg, beaten
1 c. mashed bananas
1 tsp. vanilla
1 1/2 c. flour
1/4 tsp. salt
1 tsp. soda

DIRECTIONS
…Cream shortening and sugar
well.
…Add bananas, egg, and vanilla.
…Sift salt, soda, and flour and
add to mixture.
…Beat well.
…Fill muffin tins 2/3 full.
…Bake at 375 degrees for 20
minutes.

HERB BREAD

INGREDIENTS
1 lb. butter, melted
2 tsp. basil
2 tsp. thyme
1 1/2 tsp. sage
2 tsp. marjoram
4 Tbsp. minced chives
2 loaves commercial French
  bread

DIRECTIONS
…Mix all ingredients for the
spread. Slice loaves of bread
4/5 of the way through.
…Brush mixture on both sides
of each slice.
…Wrap loaves in foil and heat
at 350 degrees for 15 minutes.

HOBO BREAD

INGREDIENTS
2 1/2 c. boiling water
2 c. raisins
4 tsp. soda
1 c. brown sugar
1 c. sugar
4 Tbsp. oil
4 c. flour
1 c. nuts, optional

DIRECTIONS
…Pour 2 1/2 cups boiling water
on raisins.
…Add soda.
…Let stand overnight.
…The next morning add brown
sugar, white sugar, oil, flour
and nuts.
…Mix well.
…Grease three 1 pound coffee cans.
…Fill to one half.
…Bake at 350 degrees for
1 hour and 10 minutes.
Makes 3 loaves.

HOLIDAY TEA SCONES

INGREDIENTS
2 c. flour
2 Tbsp. sugar
1 Tbsp. baking powder
1/2 tsp. salt
1/3 c. raisins or dried
  currants
6 Tbsp. butter
1 egg, beaten
1/2 c. milk
1 egg, slightly beaten

DIRECTIONS
…Mix together flour, sugar, baking
powder, and salt.
…Stir in raisins.
…Cut in butter until mixture resembles
coarse crumbs.
…Add 1 beaten egg and milk, stirring
just until mixture clings together.
…Knead dough gently on lightly floured
surface.
…Cut dough in half.
…Shape each half into a ball and pat or roll
into a 6 inch circle about 1/2 inch thick.
…With a sharp knife cut each circle into
6 to 8 wedges.
…Place wedges on ungreased baking sheet.
(Do not allow sides to touch.)
…Brush with slightly beaten egg.
…Bake at 425 degrees until golden brown
for 12 to 15 minutes.
Makes 12 to 16 scones.
(A unique alternative to rolls.)

IRISH SODA BREAD

INGREDIENTS

1 1/2 c. buttermilk
2 Tbsp. butter, melted
1 egg, slightly beaten
1 1/2 c. dark seedless raisins
3 c. all purpose flour
2/3 c. sugar
1 Tbsp. baking powder
1 tsp. soda
1 tsp. salt

DIRECTIONS

…In medium bowl, combine
buttermilk, butter, egg, and
raisins.
…Set aside.
…In large bowl, combine flour,
sugar, baking powder, soda, and
salt, mixing with a fork.
…Add buttermilk mixture and
mix until combined.
…Use a greased 9x5 inch loaf pan.
…Bake at 350 degrees for 50
to 55 minutes.
…Cool in pan.

HALL OF FAME ~ Every mother wants her children to be successful in their activities. When my daughter was in first-grade she won the book-reading contest and received the book of her choice as a prize. As I was about to place the book on a stand in her bedroom, my daughter said, "No! Put it in the dining room where everyone coming to the party can see it!" So I did. With this experience in mind, I let my son choose where he wanted to put his sports trophies. He chose the kitchen. I moved my private plate collection to accommodate a much more important collection and in the process made clear how important his trophies were to the rest of us. LINDA POLLY

KORNY CORN BISCUITS

INGREDIENTS

One 8 1/2 oz. can creamed yellow corn
2 c. Bisquick
1/2 c. butter

DIRECTIONS

…Stir corn and Bisquick together.
…Roll out on lightly floured surface
to 1/4 inch thickness.
…Cut into squares, triangles, or any
other shape so it does not look like a
canned biscuit.
…Melt butter in jelly roll pan.
…Coat both sides of biscuit with melted
butter and place in the same pan.
…Bake at 450 degrees until golden,
about 10 minutes.

ILLNESS IN THE FAMILY ~ When our children were about to enter 7th and 12th grade, I was diagnosed with breast cancer. From the beginning, we told our sons whatever we could about the situation. We told them that cancer did not mean death; that my diagnosis was early, so the prognosis was good. At the same time, they were prepared for the multiple trips to the doctor and hospital that treatment required. We also told them that people would be calling and asking questions, and this attention shouldn't be alarming, but rather just an expression of the concern of others. They were reminded that there are "no guarantees" in life and although the prognosis was favorable, no one knew for sure the outcome. We asked them to continue to draw upon their faith as a source of comfort and energy. As treatment was undertaken, we tried to help them rely upon their own strengths: continuing their normal routine, studying as they always had, remaining active in school activities, yet letting me rest while they contributed to maintaining a smoothly running home. We let them know each step of the way what was going on and invited them to question and share concerns. The time went very well. Neither son seems to have any scar from the family trial, but both seem decidedly attune to health issues, although not in a neurotic way. They make reasonable inquiries into family health issues. Of all the issues related to child-rearing, this is one our family handled well. DIANE GOHEEN

INGREDIENTS

1/2 c. shortening, margarine, or butter
1/2 c. sugar
1 c. milk
3 eggs, beaten
1 package instant yeast
4 1/2 c. flour

DIRECTIONS

...Measure flour and combine with yeast.
...Set aside.
...Scald milk.
...Add shortening and sugar.
...Stir until shortening is melted.
...Add eggs to milk mixture.
...Add milk mixture to flour mixture.
...Beat 3 to 5 minutes with electric mixer. (It will be sticky.)
...Refrigerate the dough at least 2 hours or up to one week.
...The dough will become firmer when it is cold.
...About 2 hours before baking, shape dough.
...Roll 1/3 of the dough into a rectangle about 3/4 inches thick.
...Spread with softened butter, cinnamon and sugar.
...Roll up starting at edge.
...Be sure to seal the edge.
...Cut 1/2 to 3/4 inch thick slices for 12 rolls.
...Let rise until they double in size.
...Bake at 375 degrees for 10 to 12 minutes.
...The entire recipe makes 3 dozen rolls.
(This dough may also be shaped into loaves or coffeecakes.)

FAVORITE FIVE MAXIMS ~ Every mother needs to keep in mind certain maxims when dealing with her children. Five of my favorites are: 1) "No" is a complete sentence. 2) If you need an answer now, the answer is "no." If I'm allowed to think about your request, I may have a different response. 3) This too shall pass. (Particularly useful with toddlers.) 4) Nothing is less important than the score at halftime. 5) Focus on the positive behaviors and praise them a lot, describing in detail what you appreciate.

LINDA VANDEGARDE

MOM NOLAN'S FAMOUS BREAD

INGREDIENTS
1/2 qt. milk
1/2 qt. potato water
1/2 c. butter
1/2 c. sugar
1/6 c. salt
1 package yeast
1 egg
2 c. flour

DIRECTIONS
…Boil the milk and potato water.
…Add the butter, sugar, and salt.
…Allow to melt.
…Melt the yeast in the mixture.
…Add egg.
…Add 2 cups of flour and beat very well with mixer.
…Continue to add extra flour until mixture is very sticky.
…Allow to rise in a large greased pan covered with a damp cloth.
…Poke dough down.
…Allow to rise again.
…At this point cut dough into loaves or make into cinnamon rolls.
…Allow to rise to twice its size.
…Bake 350 to 375 degrees until brown.

OLD FASHIONED CORN FRITTERS

INGREDIENTS
2 c. cooked corn
2 large eggs
2 to 4 Tbsp. milk
1/2 c. flour
1 tsp. baking powder
1 tsp. sugar
1 tsp. salt
Pepper
Oil for frying

DIRECTIONS
…Beat eggs.
…Add milk.
…Mix flour, baking powder, sugar, and salt.
…Mix into liquid until batter is smooth.
…Stir in corn and pepper.
…Fry batter by spoonfuls in an inch of oil over medium heat.
…Cook until crisp and brown on the bottom.
…Turn over.
…Drain on paper towels and serve hot.

OLD-TYME POPOVERS

INGREDIENTS
6 eggs, slightly beaten
2 cups milk
6 Tbsp. butter, melted
2 c. flour
1 tsp. salt

DIRECTIONS
…Blend eggs, milk, and butter.
…Gradually stir in flour and salt.
…Pour into greased popover pans or custard cups to within 1/4 inch of the top.
…Place on cookie sheet for baking.
…Bake at 375 degrees for 50 minutes.
…Slit sides with a sharp knife and return to oven until tops are firm and brown.
…Remove from pans immediately.

PISTACHIO BREAD

INGREDIENTS
1 package yellow cake mix
1 package pistachio pudding mix
8 oz. sour cream
4 eggs
1/4 c. oil
2 Tbsp. water
Topping: Your own sugar-
  cinnamon mix

DIRECTIONS
…Sprinkle 4 small loaf pans with sugar-cinnamon mixture.
…Mix cake mix, pudding mix, sour cream, eggs, oil, and water with electric mixer for two minutes until well blended.
…Pour batter into pans.
…Sprinkle top with more cinnamon-sugar mixture.
…Bake at 350 degrees for 35 to 40 minutes.
…Store in refrigerator.
(Freezes well.)

POTAWATOMI CRANBERRY BREAD

INGREDIENTS
2 c. flour
1 c. sugar
1 1/2 tsp. baking powder
1/2 tsp. soda
1 tsp. salt
1 egg, beaten
3/4 c. orange juice
3 Tbsp. orange rind, grated
3 Tbsp. oil
1/2 c. nuts
2 c. cranberries, coarsely chopped

DIRECTIONS
…Mix flour, sugar, baking powder, soda, and salt together.
…In a separate bowl combine egg, orange juice, orange rind and oil.
…Add to dry mixture, mixing only to dampen.
…Carefully fold in nuts and cranberries.
…Bake at 350 degrees for one hour.
Makes 1 loaf.

PUMPKIN BREAD

INGREDIENTS
3 1/2 c. flour
3 c. sugar
1 1/2 tsp. salt
2 tsp. soda
3 tsp. nutmeg
3 tsp. cinnamon
4 eggs
1 c. oil
2/3 c. water
1 can pumpkin

DIRECTIONS
...Mix flour, sugar, salt, soda, nutmeg, and cinnamon.
...Add eggs, oil, water, and pumpkin.
...Pour into 3 loaf pans and bake at 325 degrees for 50 to 60 minutes.

QUICK BLUEBERRY SCONES

INGREDIENTS
3 c. Bisquick
1/4 c. sugar
1 1/2 tsp. grated lemon peel
1 c. fresh or frozen blueberries
3 eggs
1/4 c. milk

DIRECTIONS
...In a bowl combine baking mix, 2 Tbsp. sugar, lemon peel, and blueberries.
...Beat eggs with milk and blend into mix with a fork.
...Drop onto baking sheet.
...Sprinkle with sugar.
...Bake in 400 degree oven for 10 to 12 minutes until browned.
(May be doubled.)
Makes 12 scones.

TEENAGE BUDGET ~ When

my two girls were teenagers they always wanted the latest clothing fad just like everyone else their age. To try and reign in their impulse to shop they were offered the opportunity to be on a weekly allowance, which was intended to be enough for school lunches, entertainment, and all their clothes, except for shoes and coats. They accepted this offer with great excitement, and visions, I'm sure, of bulging closets and drawers. (Of course, the allowance did not provide for this.) The result was they each found a way to extend their allowance. One of them was a beautiful seamstress and made all her clothes during high school. The other one worked a part time job. They both became thrifty shoppers, a talent that benefits them to this day. JO HALLEY

RANCH BREAD

INGREDIENTS

3/4 c. water
1/4 c. honey
2 Tbsp. molasses
1/3 c. shortening
1/4 c. oats
1/4 c. sesame seeds
1/3 c. cracked wheat
1/4 c. corn meal
2/3 c. dry milk
5 tsp. yeast
2 1/4 c. whole wheat
  flour
5 c. white flour
1 Tbsp. salt

DIRECTIONS

...Heat the first 4 ingredients to a boil.
...Put oats, sesame seeds, cracked wheat, and corn meal in an electric mixer.
...Add 2 1/2 cups water to the liquid mixture to reduce temperature to luke warm.
...Pour over dry mixture.
...Add whole wheat flour, 1 tsp. salt, white flour, and yeast dissolved in 1/3 c. water.
...Mix in electric mixer and then knead dough on lightly floured board.
...Place in large greased bowl.
...Let it rise in a warm place until double in size.
...Separate into 3 greased loaf pans.
...Let rise again.
...Bake at 350 degrees for 40 minutes.
(You may add 1 to 2 eggs for added flavor and texture.)

STUDY "POWER" ~ When report cards arrived, and they did not meet our expectations we started having "power outages." Between the hours of 7:00 and 9:00pm there was a "blackout" — no T.V., phone, C.D. player, or computer chats! This really seemed to work at our house, especially if Mom and Dad had to suffer the same fate.

PAT DARNALL

SIX-WEEK-SALE BRAN MUFFINS

INGREDIENTS

One 15 oz. box bran flakes
   with raisins
3 c. sugar
5 c. flour
5 tsp. soda
1 tsp. salt
4 eggs, beaten
1 c. oil
1 qt. buttermilk

DIRECTIONS

…Mix cereal, sugar, flour, soda, and salt.
…Add eggs, shortening, and milk.
…Refrigerate in covered container.
…To bake, fill paper muffin cups 2/3 full.
…Bake at 400 degrees for 15 minutes.
Makes 7 dozen.

STEPHENSON'S RESTAURANT FRESH APPLE FRITTERS

INGREDIENTS

1 c. milk
1 egg, beaten
1/4 c. butter
1/2 c. powdered sugar
1/2 tsp. salt
1 c. orange juice and rind
1 c. apple, finely chopped
3 c. flour
2 tsp. baking powder
1 tsp. vanilla

DIRECTIONS

…In a bowl combine beaten egg, milk, and melted butter.
…Add orange juice, orange rind, unpeeled apple, and vanilla.
…Add flour, salt, and baking powder and stir with a spoon until blended.
…Do not over mix.
…Preheat oil in skillet to 350 degrees.
…Drop dough by tsp. into hot oil.
…Fry to golden brown.
…Turn so they are even in color.
…Cool.
…Roll in powdered sugar.
…Serve as bread or as a dessert.
Makes 40 fritters.

MOTHERING THE IN-LAWS ~ Sometimes we must "parent" someone other than our children. Many friends have joined me over the years in the annual family challenge of where to spend the holidays. Long drives across the Midwest with small children in the winter can be very dangerous. After one frightening car trip through a five-state blizzard I returned home from the in-laws determined to develop a new set of holiday plans. My husband and I both agreed that we could not take this risk again. My "light bulb moment" was when I realized this new idea would meet with much less resistance if their son explained our future travel and vacation plans to them. I took myself out of the triangle and the conflict. I never picked up the phone during these conversations. It was his responsibility to explain our decision to them and mine to explain it to my own parents. I remember this lesson now that my own children are grown and live across the country. They have limited vacation time and are very busy young adults. I encourage them to travel to as many new places as they can. So when they come to our home to visit, I know they are coming to enjoy the comforts they remember from childhood, not out of obligation. LINDA POLLY

SWEDISH LYMPA BREAD

INGREDIENTS
2 packages dry yeast
5 c. rye flour
2 c. white flour
1/2 c. orange juice
1 /2 c. warm water
1/2 c. oil
2 eggs
1/2 c. molasses
1/2 c. honey
1 Tbsp. salt
1 grated orange rind

DIRECTIONS
…Dissolve yeast in 1 c. warm water.
…Let it stand for 10 minutes.
…Beat in 2 cups white flour until mixture is smooth.
…Add orange juice, 1/2 c. warm water, oil, eggs, molasses, honey, salt, and rind.
…Blend very well.
…Mix in rye flour, 1 c. at a time, until dough is manageable.
…Kneed on well-floured surface for 10 minutes.
…Put dough in a large buttered bowl in the oven (without heat).
…Let rise until double in size, about 1 1/2 hours.
…Transfer into two greased loaf pans, rolled with seams on the bottom, and return to oven until doubled in size again.
…Leave in oven for one hour.
…Remove pans.
…Preheat oven to 375 degrees.
…Bake for one hour.
…Remove loaves from pans and cool.

TIPPIN'S CORN BREAD

INGREDIENTS
1 box Jiffy corn bread mix
1 box Jiffy yellow cake mix
1/3 c. milk
1/3 c. water
2 eggs
1/4 c. oil

DIRECTIONS
…Mix corn bread mix, cake mix, milk, water, eggs, and oil.
…Mix together until moist.
…Pour into 8x8 greased pan.
…Bake at 400 degrees for 5 minutes.
…Reduce heat to 350 degrees and bake for 20 to 25 minutes.

WILMA'S SAUSAGE BREAD

INGREDIENTS
1 loaf frozen bread
1 lb. sausage
2 eggs
1 c. Parmesan cheese

DIRECTIONS
…Thaw bread dough and roll out flat.
…Cook and drain sausage.
…Mix sausage, eggs and cheese.
…Fill center of bread.
…Fold dough over and seal edges tightly. Allow to rise.
…Bake at 350 degrees for 30 to 45 minutes or until bread is brown.
…Slice and serve.

WISCONSIN BEER BREAD

INGREDIENTS
3 c. self rising flour
1/3 c. sugar
One 12 oz. can beer, at room temperature
2 to 3 Tbsp. melted butter

DIRECTIONS
…Mix flour, sugar, and beer to form a thick batter.
…Spoon into a greased loaf pan.
…Cover and let rise at room temperature for one hour.
…Brush the top with half the melted butter.
…Bake at 350 degrees for one hour.
…Brush top with remaining butter.
…Serve warm.

ZUCCHINI BREAD

INGREDIENTS
3 eggs, beaten
1 c. oil
2 c. sugar
2 c. zucchini, grated
3 c. flour
1 tsp. soda
1/2 tsp. baking powder
1 tsp. salt
1 tsp. cinnamon
1/2 c. nuts
2 tsp. vanilla

DIRECTIONS
…Cream eggs, oil, sugar, zucchini, and vanilla.
…Sift together flour, salt, soda, cinnamon, and baking powder.
…Add to egg mixture.
…Stir in nuts.
…Pour into two loaf pans.
…Bake at 350 degrees for 55 minutes.

CASSEROLES CASSEROLES CASSEROLES CASSEROLES CASSEROLES CASSEROLES CASSEROLES CASSERO

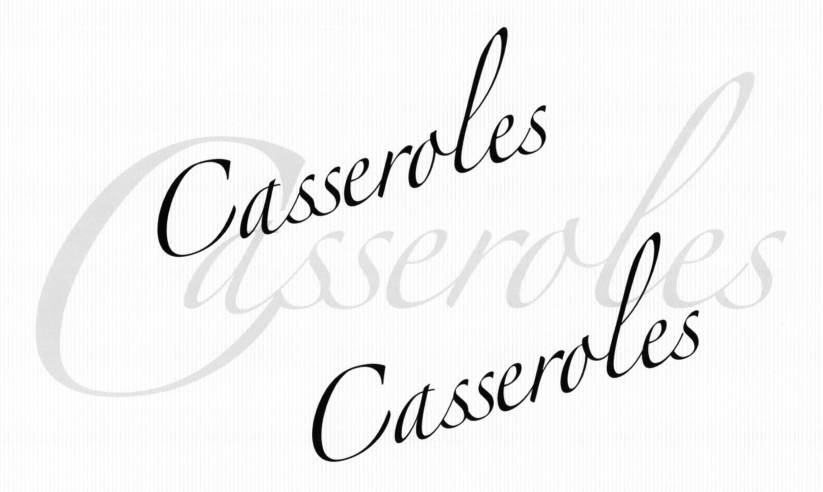

Casseroles

Casseroles

CASSEROLES CASSEROLES CASSEROLES CASSEROLES CASSEROLES CASSEROLES CASSEROLES CASSEROLES CASSEROLES CASSEROLES CASSEROLES CASSEROLES CASSEROLES CASSEROLES CASSEROLES CASSEROLES CASSEROLES

READ EARLY AND OFTEN ~ Don't wait until your child is six months old. Start early. Set aside a special time for this bonding experience. Save your children's books! Never sell them. Make trips to the public library a special treat! Gift subscriptions to magazines such as *Ranger Rick* are good suggestions for grandparents and godparents. But when the magazines arrive, don't let them pile up or expect your children to enjoy them on their own, especially when they are young. I have been a teacher for many years, and I know this works. Children long for one-on-one time with their parents. JANE BOLDENOW

ADOBE CHICKEN CASSEROLE

INGREDIENTS

2 lb. chicken breasts, cooked and cubed
4 Tbsp. butter
1 c. onion, chopped
3 Tbsp. flour
2 c. milk
1 1/2 tsp. salt
1 lb. sharp cheddar cheese, grated
One 10 oz. can Ro-Tel tomatoes with green chilies
12 corn tortillas, torn into small pieces
1 c. chicken broth
One 4 oz. can green chilies, seeded and chopped

DIRECTIONS

...Sauté onion in butter.
...Add flour and cook until bubbly.
...Add milk and chicken broth and stir until thick.
...Add chilies and tomatoes.
...Place a layer of chicken in bottom of a buttered 3 qt. casserole.
...Add a layer of tortillas, cheese, and sauce.
...Repeat layers with cheese on top.
...Bake at 375 degrees until bubbly.
(May be prepared ahead and frozen.)
Serves 8.

ASPARAGUS-SHRIMP CASSEROLE

INGREDIENTS
One 1 lb. can green asparagus
24 saltine crackers, crushed
4 hard boiled eggs, sliced
1 lb. boiled shrimp
1 c. milk
1 Tbsp. minced onion
1/4 lb. cheddar cheese, grated
1/4 c. butter
1 can cream of mushroom soup

DIRECTIONS
…Grease 2 qt. casserole dish.
…Drain asparagus.
…Place one half of cracker crumbs in bottom of casserole.
…Place asparagus, eggs and shrimp in layers.
…Top with cheese and remaining crumbs.
…Dot with butter.
…Bake at 325 degrees for 45 minutes.
…Let rest 20 minutes before serving.
Serves 8.

BASIC CREPES

INGREDIENTS
1 1/2 c. milk
2 Tbsp. butter
3 eggs
1 1/2 c. flour
1/4 tsp. salt
2 Tbsp. oil

DIRECTIONS
…Beat eggs well.
…Add dry ingredients, alternating with milk and oil.
…Beat until smooth.
…Stir before using.
…Serve with luncheon or dessert filling.
(Batter may be refrigerated for up to 3 days.)
Makes 24 crepes.

CURFEW ~ Having two, then three, then four teenagers at the same time — in order to get my beauty sleep and keep my sunny disposition — I set my alarm for the curfew hour of 12:30am. If my alarm went off, I got up and started waiting and worrying. This was very effective in our home, because you know the old saying, "When mom ain't happy, ain't nobody happy." MARY ALICE MCRAE

CURFEW RULES FOR EVERYONE ~ Different
children respond to family rules differently, especially as
they get older. This was true in our case when it came to
curfew. Our oldest son never had a problem getting home
on time, but our older daughter felt her curfew in high
school was too early. We were eventually able to settle on
a compromise: "call and negotiate." If she felt she needed
more time, she would call, explain where she was, what she
was doing, and with whom. I would weigh this information
and usually grant a curfew extension, which she always
honored. It turned out she didn't feel the need to use
"call and negotiate" very often, but it gave her a feeling of
freedom, and me a more peaceful night, right up until the
moment I heard the key in the lock. MARILYN UNREIN

BLUEBERRY FRENCH TOAST CASSEROLE

INGREDIENTS
12 slices day-old bread, cut into
  one-inch cubes
Two 8 oz. packages cream cheese,
  cubed
1 c. fresh or frozen blueberries
12 eggs
2 c. milk
1/2 c. granulated sugar
1/3 c. honey

DIRECTIONS
…Preheat oven to 350 degrees.
…Spread half of bread cubes in
9x13 casserole.
…Sprinkle cream cheese cubes
evenly over bread and sprinkle
with blueberries.
…Top with remaining bread cubes.
…In a medium sized bowl, beat
eggs, milk, sugar, and honey with
a whisk.
…Pour evenly over bread.
…Cover and refrigerate overnight.
…Bake covered for 45 minutes.
…Remove cover and bake an
additional 25 to 30 minutes.

BLUEBERRY FRENCH TOAST SAUCE

INGREDIENTS
2 c. sugar
4 Tbsp. cornstarch
2 c. cold water
2 c. blueberries
2 Tbsp. butter

DIRECTIONS
…Make the sauce while
French toast is baking.
…Boil sugar, cornstarch, and
water in a saucepan.
…Add blueberries and butter.
…Reduce heat and simmer
for 10 minutes.
…Serve over French toast.
8 servings.

CHICKEN AND CHEESE ENCHILADAS

INGREDIENTS
6 chicken breasts
1 onion
3 carrots
3 stalks celery
Garlic salt
Pepper
Flour tortillas
1 bunch scallions
2 cloves garlic
1 tsp. oil
1 c. cheddar cheese, grated
1 c. Jack cheese, grated
1 can cream of chicken soup
8 oz. package cream cheese, cubed
1 can chopped green chilies

DIRECTIONS
…Poach chicken with onion, celery,
carrots, garlic salt and pepper.
…Cool and chop.
…Sauté scallions and garlic in oil until
soft.
…Mix chicken with all ingredients
except the cheddar cheese.
…Heat oil in a skillet.
…Dip tortillas in the oil to soften.
…Place 1/2 c. of chicken mixture on
tortilla.
…Roll up and place on baking sheet.
…Bake at 325 degrees for 30 minutes.
…Sprinkle cheese on top during the
last 5 minutes of baking.

CHORE LIST ~ I'm a big believer in the daily chore list. I keep it on the refrigerator so it is in plain sight. Next to each chore is a box which my children can check off when they are finished. This places the responsibility on them. It also keeps mom from continually asking them to "Pick up!" "Put away!" "Do this!" "Do that!" Before bedtime, I check the list. If there is no initial, then there are consequences. But if they have a great week, they are rewarded with a treat: pizza, movie, ice cream, etc. It has worked for our family. The children learn how to take responsibility for their behavior and mom learns how to nag less.

TERESA O'NEAL

CHICKEN ARTICHOKE CASSEROLE

INGREDIENTS
1 package Rice-a-Roni chicken flavored rice mix, cooked as directed
2 c. cooked chicken, cubed
2 jars marinated artichoke hearts, undrained
4 scallions, including tops, chopped
1 c. mayonnaise
1/2 tsp. curry powder
1 can sliced water chestnuts, halved

DIRECTIONS
...Mix all ingredients together.
...Serve as a cold casserole or bake at 350 degrees for 25 to 30 minutes for hot entree.
Serves 6.

CHICKEN CHINESE CASSEROLE

INGREDIENTS
2 cans cream of mushroom soup
1/2 c. water
2 c. chopped chicken
1/2 c. chopped onion
2 c. celery
1 c. Chinese noodles
5 oz. cashews

DIRECTIONS
...Combine soup, water, chicken, onion, and celery.
...Pour into greased baking pan.
...Sprinkle top with noodles, and cashews.
...Bake for one hour at 350 degrees.
Serves 6.

CHICKEN PUFFS

INGREDIENTS

1 can boned chicken (if doubling
    recipe, boil and bone 2 1/2 lb.
    fryer)
One 8 oz. package cream cheese
One 2 oz. jar mushroom pieces
1 can of 8 crescent rolls
1/2 c. breadcrumbs
1/2 c. finely chopped walnuts or
    pecans (optional)
3 Tbsp. butter, melted
1/2 tsp. lemon juice
Salt and pepper

DIRECTIONS

…Combine breadcrumbs and
nuts and set aside.
…Combine soft cream cheese,
chicken, mushrooms, lemon juice,
salt and pepper.
…Separate crescent rolls.
…Spread thin enough to wrap
around chicken mixture.
…Drop 1/4 c. chicken mixture on
each roll.
…Bring edges of rolls around and
press to seal.
…Dip ball into melted butter and
roll in crumbs.
…Place on ungreased cookie
sheet.
…Bake at 350 degrees for 15 to 20
minutes.
Serves 8.

COUNTRY CRESCENT BACON BRUNCH

INGREDIENTS

12 slices bacon, fried and crumbled
One 8 oz. can crescent rolls
3 eggs, slightly beaten
3/4 c. milk
1 Tbsp. instant minced onion
2 Tbsp. chopped parsley flakes
1/2 c. Swiss cheese, shredded

DIRECTIONS

…Spread out crescent roll dough on
an ungreased 14 inch pizza pan.
…Press the pieces together and
form an edge all around the pan
with the dough.
…Mix the beaten eggs, milk, onion,
and parsley flakes together and
pour onto the dough.
…Sprinkle crumbled bacon and
Swiss cheese on top.
…Bake at 425 degrees for 18 to 20
minutes.
…Slice as you would a pizza.

COUNTY FAIR SPAGHETTI PIE

INGREDIENTS

Crust:
6 oz. cooked spaghetti
1/2 c. Parmesan cheese
2 eggs, beaten
Mix together and form into
    10 inch pie plate

Filling:
1 lb. ground beef
1/2 c. onion, chopped
1/2 c. green pepper, chopped
One 7 oz. can tomatoes
One 6 oz. can tomato paste
1 tsp. sugar
1/2 tsp. garlic salt

Topping:
1 c. cottage cheese
1/2 c. mozzarella cheese,
    shredded

DIRECTIONS

…Fry meat and drain.
…Combine with other filling ingredients and heat.
…Spread cottage cheese over spaghetti crust.
…Fill pie shell with tomato-meat mixture.
…Bake uncovered at 350 degrees for 20 minutes.
…Sprinkle with mozzarella cheese and bake for additional 5 minutes or until cheese melts.

CURFEW ~ As they grew older, it seemed my children were continually out with their friends. Instead of asking them where they were going or who they were out with, I asked them to draw me a map so that I would know "in which ditch" to look for them if they did not arrive home at a reasonable time. It worked! I can still see the faces of my sons' peers as they sat drawing me a map so that I might look in ditches along the road if they did not make it home by curfew. "You are doing what?" they would say. BETTY CLELAND

ENCHILADAS VERDES – CALIFORNIA STYLE

INGREDIENTS

Green Sauce:
Two 11 oz. can tomatillos
1 medium onion, chopped
1/4 c. olive oil
1/4 c. almonds, finely chopped
2 cloves garlic, minced
One 4 oz. can diced
  green chilies
2 cups chicken broth

Filling:
Meat from 1 stewed chicken
  (use broth in green sauce.)
12 flour tortillas
1 onion, chopped
1 1/2 c. Jack cheese, grated
1/2 c. fresh cilantro, chopped

DIRECTIONS

…Sauté onion in olive oil in a large skillet until golden.
…Add garlic for one minute.
…Add pureed tomatillos (tart Mexican vegetable found in most well stocked supermarkets or Latin American markets), chilies, almonds, and chicken broth.
…Simmer 10 minutes until slightly thickened.
…Preheat oven to 325 degrees.
…Fill tortillas with chicken, onion, cheese, and cilantro.
…Roll up.
…Place seam side down in a 9x13 casserole.
…Pour green sauce on top and warm in oven for 30 minutes.
…Serve with guacamole, sour cream, corn salsa, and pico de gallo.
Serves 6.

ÉTOUFFÉE

INGREDIENTS

1/4 lb. margarine
1 bell pepper, chopped
1 can Ro-Tel tomatoes
3 onions, chopped
4 scallions, chopped
4 celery stalks, chopped
Juice of 1/2 lemon
2 cloves garlic, minced
Parsley
1 can cream of mushroom soup
2 lb. raw shrimp, peeled and deveined
Dash Worcestershire sauce
Sherry, optional

DIRECTIONS

…Simmer margarine, pepper, tomatoes, onions, and celery for two or more hours.
…Add lemon, garlic, Worcestershire sauce, and parsley.
…Mix well and add shrimp.
…Simmer 5 to 10 minutes or until shrimp turns pink.
…Add sherry if mixture needs thinning.
…Serve over rice.
Serves 6.

FARMER'S CORN CASSEROLE

INGREDIENTS
1 egg
1/2 c. butter, softened
3/4 c. sour cream
One 17 oz. can whole kernel
 corn, drained
17 oz. can cream-style corn
1/4 tsp. salt
1/2 c. milk
One 8 oz. box corn muffin mix
1 c. cheddar cheese, shredded

DIRECTIONS
…In a large bowl beat egg.
…Add butter and sour cream
and mix well.
…Stir in the drained corn, cream
style corn, salt, and milk.
…Add the corn muffin mix.
…Mix well.
…Pour mixture into lightly
greased 9 inch baking dish.
…Top with cheese.
…Bake uncovered at 350 degrees
 for 40 to 45 minutes.
Serves 6.

HOT CHICKEN CASSEROLE

INGREDIENTS
8 chicken breasts, cooked and cubed
1 1/2 tsp. salt
4 c. celery, diced
1 c. almonds, toasted
4 Tbsp. onion, grated
4 tsp. lemon juice
1/2 lb. cheddar cheese, grated
Two 8 oz. cans mushrooms, drained
1 can water chestnuts, drained
2 1/2 c. mayonnaise

DIRECTIONS
…Fold all ingredients together.
…Pour into 9x13 casserole dish.
…Bake at 400 degrees until bubbly,
approximately 30 to 45 minutes.
Serves 12.
(Good for luncheons.)

HOT CHICKEN SALAD EN CROTE

INGREDIENTS

3 c. cooked chicken
1 can cream of chicken soup
2/3 c. mayonnaise
1/2 c. chopped celery
One 4 oz. can mushrooms
1/2 c. sour cream
One 8 oz. jar water chestnuts, drained
1 package crescent rolls
12 slivered almonds
1/4 c. butter, melted
2/3 c. Swiss cheese, shredded

DIRECTIONS

…Mix chicken, soup, mayonnaise, celery, mushrooms, sour cream, and water chestnuts together. Pour into a greased 9x13 casserole dish.
…Top with the crescent rolls.
…Sprinkle on the Swiss cheese, almonds, and butter.
…Bake at 350 degrees for 30 to 45 minutes or until crust is golden.
Serves 8.

MOTHER'S CHEESE PUDDING

INGREDIENTS

8 slices white bread
Soft butter
1 lb. Velveeta cheese, sliced
4 eggs
2 1/2 c. milk
1 tsp. salt
1/4 tsp. dry mustard
1/2 c. shredded cheddar cheese

DIRECTIONS

…Preheat oven to 325 degrees.
…Butter a soufflé dish.
…Butter bread and cut into fourths at right angles.
…Then cut into eighths by cutting on diagonals to each corner of the slice of bread.
…Layer buttered bread pieces and cheese slices in dish, beginning and ending with bread.
…Beat eggs, milk, salt, and mustard together.
…Pour over bread and cheese.
…Sprinkle cheddar cheese over top.
…Bake 45 minutes.
Serves 6 to 8.

NEWPORT EGGS

INGREDIENTS

1 can cream of chicken soup
1 can cream of mushroom soup
1 c. mayonnaise
2 tsp. lemon juice
3 Tbsp. sherry
1/2 c. milk
1 lb. sausage
12 eggs, hard boiled

DIRECTIONS

…Brown and drain sausage.
…Mix soups, mayonnaise, lemon juice, sherry and milk for the sauce.
…Cover the bottom of a 9x13 casserole dish with one half of the sauce.
…Cut eggs in half and place yellow side up in sauce.
…Sprinkle sausage over eggs.
…Top with remaining sauce.
…Bake at 350 degrees for 20 to 30 minutes.
Serves 8 to 10.

OEUFS ENTRAILLES (HARD BOILED EGG CASSEROLE)

INGREDIENTS

1 1/2 dozen boiled eggs, sliced
1/2 lb. bacon
1/4 c. butter
1/4 c. flour
1 c. light cream (half and half)
1 c. milk
1 lb. sharp or medium cheddar
   cheese, grated
1/2 tsp. salt, dash pepper
1 clove garlic, crushed
1/4 tsp. thyme
1/4 tsp. marjoram
1/4 tsp. chopped parsley
1 1/2 to 2 c. buttered
   breadcrumbs

DIRECTIONS

...Fry bacon until crisp.
...Drain and crumble.
...Make a cream sauce using butter,
flour, cream, and milk.
...Add cheese and stir until cheese is
melted.
...Season with all spices.
...Layer bacon crumbs, egg slices, and
1/3 cream.
...Continue until all ingredients are
used, ending with sauce.
...Sprinkle with breadcrumbs.
...Bake for 20 minutes in 9x13 casserole
dish or until crumbs are lightly
browned and the mixture is bubbly.
Serves 12.

SAUSAGE SOUFFLÉ

INGREDIENTS

8 eggs
8 slices French bread, cubed
4 c. milk
2 Tbsp. salt
2 tsp. dry mustard
1/2 lb. sausage, browned
   and drained
1 c. Swiss cheese, grated

DIRECTIONS

...Butter 9x13 casserole dish.
...Layer bottom with bread.
...Sprinkle sausage over bread.
...Add cheese.
...Mix eggs, milk, salt, and
mustard together.
...Pour over casserole.
...Refrigerate overnight.
...Bake at 375 degrees for
30 minutes.
Serves 8.

PACIFIERS ~ If you listen to your child, often they will come up with the way to solve their own problems. Our daughter, Jennifer, walked early, talked early, and by the age of two was about the most adorable and clever little girl in Kansas, in the humble opinion of her mother. But, the one area that remained a real problem was that she used a pacifier to go to sleep: her "binky." Only the binky would work, but we lived a long way from a "binky store" that sold the proper model, which I bought literally by the box. No binky meant no sleep for Jennifer or her parents. So her educated, adult parents brainstormed various stratagems for eliminating the "binky", all to no avail. As Christmas and her third birthday approached, Jenni approached us with wide-eyed excitement, "Let's leave the binky out for Santa to take to a new baby!" So with much planning, we put out the binky with the cookies and milk for Santa. She actually went to sleep that night without it. Her awe the next morning that the binky was gone, along with the other treats, was inspiring. Santa left a note thanking her for her gift. She still missed the binky but was comforted that Santa had a better use for it. She told everyone that Santa had taken her binky to a new baby. As our family slept peacefully after that, we understood the real meaning of Christmas. LEAH GABLER-MARSHALL

SMOKED SALMON PASTA

INGREDIENTS
8 oz. linguine or fettuccine
1/2 c. butter
1 c. sour cream
2 tsp. ground garlic
1 egg, slightly beaten
1/2 c. Parmesan cheese
2/3 c. chopped tomatoes, peeled, and seeded
4 to 6 oz. smoked salmon
1 Tbsp. chives, chopped
1 Tbsp. minced parsley

DIRECTIONS
…Cook pasta in boiling water al dente.
…Drain.
…Melt butter in separate pan.
…Stir in sour cream, garlic, egg, and 1/4 c. Parmesan cheese.
…Fold in tomatoes, smoked salmon pieces and chives.
…Season with salt and pepper.
…Fold sauce into hot pasta.
…Pour onto serving platter and garnish with remaining Parmesan cheese and parsley.
Serves 8.

SPICY PASTA CASSEROLE

INGREDIENTS
1 lb. fine egg noodles
  or vermicelli
2 c. cottage cheese
3 c. sour cream
2 cloves garlic, minced
2 onions, chopped
2 Tbsp. Worcestershire sauce
Dash liquid hot pepper
  seasoning
2 Tbsp. horseradish
1 c. Parmesan cheese, divided
Additional sour cream

DIRECTIONS
…Cook noodles in boiling water.
…Drain.
…In a large bowl mix all ingredients except Parmesan cheese and additional sour cream.
…Add noodles and mix.
…Pour into 4 qt. buttered casserole.
…Cover and bake at 350 degrees for 40 minutes.
…Remove cover and add 1/4 c. Parmesan cheese.
…Place under broiler until cheese browns.
…Serve with additional cheese and sour cream.
Serves 8.

STUFFED FRENCH TOAST STRATA

INGREDIENTS

One 1 lb. loaf French bread
One 8 oz. package cream cheese, cubed
8 eggs
2 1/2 c. milk or half and half
6 Tbsp. butter, melted
1/4 c. maple syrup

DIRECTIONS

…Cut French bread into cubes (makes about twelve cups).
…Put 1/2 of bread cubes into a greased 9x13 pan.
…Top with cream cheese cubes and the remaining bread cubes.
…Mix eggs, milk, butter, and syrup until well blended.
…Pour mixture evenly over bread.
…Press down to moisten bread.
…Cover and refrigerate for 6 to 24 hours.
…Bake at 325 degrees uncovered for 35 to 40 minutes.
…Let rest 10 minutes.
…Serve with pure maple syrup.
Serves 8.

THANK YOU NOTES ~ As a mother, I tried to teach my children to always be appreciative when receiving gifts. It makes both the giving and receiving so much more gratifying and the gifts themselves priceless! There's no doubt we spoiled our children, but they always knew that the gifts they received were just that — gifts — not something that anyone owed them. They usually spent the week after birthdays and Christmas writing thank you notes. This was not by choice, I might add, but because it was a daily requirement until the task was completed. They've grown up to become responsible and compassionate adults, who continue to be grateful and appreciative for all they receive. And yes, they both still write thank you notes, and I have no doubt will teach their children to do the same.

PAM FERRELL

SUNDAY BRUNCH QUICHE

INGREDIENTS
1 c. ham, shredded
1 c. Swiss cheese, shredded
3 eggs
1 c. milk
1 tsp. nutmeg
1 tsp. dry mustard
1 tsp. flour
1 pastry shell
Salt and pepper to taste

DIRECTIONS
…Layer meat and cheese in a pastry shell. Mix eggs, milk, nutmeg, mustard, and flour. Pour into pie shell.
…Bake at 350 degrees for 30 to 35 minutes.
(You may substitute bacon or sausage for the ham to vary the recipe.)
Serves 6.

SUNRISE CASSEROLE

INGREDIENTS
1 lb. sausage, regular or hot
Two 4 oz. packages plain or green pepper hash browns
(if plain potatoes are used, add 1 chopped onion and green pepper)
1 can cream of celery soup
1 1/2 c. milk
1 1/2 c. diced Velveeta cheese
7 eggs, beaten

DIRECTIONS
…Brown, drain, and crumble sausage.
…Add potatoes, soup, milk, cheese, and eggs.
…Pour into 13x9 casserole dish.
…Bake at 350 degrees for 40 to 60 minutes or until done.
…May be made the day ahead and refrigerated.
(This is a good football game day dish.)
Serves 8.

TRAIL DRIVE MACARONI & CHEESE

INGREDIENTS
2 c. uncooked macaroni
1 stick butter
12 oz. cheddar cheese, shredded
5 c. milk
Salt and pepper

DIRECTIONS
…Preheat oven to 350 degrees.
…Layer macaroni, butter, and cheese in a 9x13 casserole.
…Pour milk over the top.
…Bake uncovered for one hour.
(This is a great recipe to make with children when they are starting to learn to cook.)
Serves 8.

VELVETY CHICKEN CASSEROLE

INGREDIENTS
Two 8 oz. jars artichoke hearts
1 pint fresh mushrooms
2 c. cooked chicken
1 envelope chicken gravy mix
1/4 tsp. crushed marjoram
4 oz. Swiss cheese, shredded
2 Tbsp. sherry

Topping:
3/4 c. breadcrumbs
2 Tbsp. melted butter

DIRECTIONS
...Cook artichokes according to
package directions.
...Drain.
...Cook mushrooms in butter
until tender.
...Combine artichokes, mushrooms,
and chicken in a 2 qt. casserole.
...Make chicken gravy according
to package directions.
...Add marjoram and cheese to gravy.
...Stir until cheese melts.
...Add sherry.
...Mix sauce with chicken in casserole.
...Sprinkle with topping.
...Bake uncovered at 375 degrees
for 30 minutes.
Serves 6.

WELSH RAREBIT

INGREDIENTS
1/2 lb. sharp cheddar cheese
3/4 c. cream
1 tsp. Worcestershire sauce
1/2 tsp. mustard
4 slices bread, toasted

DIRECTIONS
...Melt cheese in the top of a
double boiler.
...Add cream gradually, stirring
constantly.
...Add seasoning.
...When very hot pour over toast.
...Serves 4.
(This makes a nice light luncheon
or supper dish.)

BEEF PORK VENISON & LAMB BEEF PORK VENISON & LAMB BEEF PORK VENISON & LAMB BEEF

Beef, Pork, Venison & Lamb

BEEF PORK VENISON & LAMB BEEF PORK VENISON & LAMB BEEF PORK VENISON & LAMB BEEF PORK VENISON & LAMB BEEF PORK VENISON & LAMB BEEF PORK VENISON & LAMB BEEF PORK VENISON & LAMB BEEF PORK VENISON & LAMB & LAMB

DIARY FOR YOUR CHILDREN ~
I know many mothers who keep a daily journal for themselves, but how many keep a journal for their children? For our family, it started with their grandparents who stayed with our children when we went on vacation alone (very important to keep the marriage happy). We asked the grandparents to keep a journal of what our children said and did, so we could experience what we had missed. This is how the diary began. I started to keep it after that. After a few years, I realized that my kids, when they were adults, would enjoy reading what they said when they were young more than what I said. LINDA POLLY

THE SPECIAL PLATE ~ I asked a father of five very successful children how he did it. He said his parenting style followed the lines of the old song: "Accentuate the positive and ignore the negative…." I instituted the "Red Plate" tradition to mark our children's special achievements. The Red Plate is sold in most department stores. "You Are Special Today" is written in large white script around the border of this red plate. When one of our children achieved something special (i.e. making the ball team, excellent grades, publishing), he or she received the red plate for dinner. During the meal we let Dad try to guess why the plate had been awarded, and then the celebration began. Given all of our busy schedules, we were not always able to eat dinner together but on Red Plate nights, we had a much longer and fancier meal together. LINDA POLLY

BEEF

DODGE CITY BEEF WELLINGTON

INGREDIENTS
8 beef filets, 5 oz.
Salad oil
Pate, 8 oz.
Salt and pepper
8 frozen pastry shells, thawed
1 slightly beaten egg white

DIRECTIONS
…Place filets in freezer for 20 minutes.
…Remove and brush with salad oil.
…Season with salt and pepper.
…Sear in skillet for 5 minutes on each side.
…Spread one ounce of pate on each filet.
…Roll out each pastry shell to 9 x 5 x 1/8 inch.
…Place filet with pate on the bottom in the middle of the rolled out shell.
…Bring up the sides of the dough and seal.
…Place Beef Wellingtons seam side down in a shallow pan and refrigerate.
…Before baking brush with the beaten egg white.
…Bake at 450 degrees.
…10 minutes for rare; 12 minutes for medium rare, 15 minutes for medium.
…Serve with béarnaise sauce.
Serves 8.

BEEF TENDERLOIN

INGREDIENTS
4 to 5 lb. tenderloin
Fresh cracked pepper
Steak seasoning

DIRECTIONS
…Season all sides of tenderloin with pepper and steak seasoning.
…Bake uncovered at 450 degrees for 40 to 45 minutes.
…Remove from oven.
…Cover with foil and allow meat to rest for 30 minutes.
…Slice and serve.
Serves 8 to 10.

HEREFORD FLANK STEAK

INGREDIENTS
2 lb. flank steak
2/3 c. beer
1/3 c. oil
1 Tbsp. salt
1/4 tsp. garlic
1/4 tsp. pepper

DIRECTIONS
…Place steak in glass dish.
…Add all other ingredients.
…Cover and refrigerate for 1 to
2 days.
(This meat, when grilled, can be
used for fajitas, sliced with sautéed
onions and its juice for hoagies, or
with your favorite pasta.)
Serves 4.

KANSAS BRISKET 1

INGREDIENTS
3 to 5 lbs. brisket of beef
2 Tbsp. liquid smoke
2 Tbsp. soy sauce
2 tsp. celery seed
2 tsp. garlic cloves, chopped
1 tsp. onion salt
1/4 c. water

DIRECTIONS
…Combine liquid smoke, soy
sauce, celery seed, garlic, onion
salt and water.
…In a baking pan with sides
large enough to hold the beef,
place a large sheet of heavy
aluminum foil.
…Place brisket in foil and pour the
combined ingredients over the beef.
…Fold and seal the foil.
…Marinate in refrigerator
overnight.
…Bake 5 hours at 300 degrees.
…Do not open oven door during
baking.
Serves 8.

KANSAS BRISKET 2

INGREDIENTS
5 lb. brisket
2 Tbsp. Worcestershire sauce
1 tsp. garlic salt
1 tsp. pepper
2 Tbsp. liquid smoke
1 tsp. celery salt
1 tsp. onion salt
1 1/2 c. barbecue sauce

DIRECTIONS
…Place meat in a pan lined
with aluminum foil.
…Poke holes in meat.
…Pour liquid smoke and
Worcestershire sauce over brisket.
…Sprinkle dry ingredients
over meat.
…Seal foil around meat and
marinate 10 hours.
…Bake 5 hours at 300 degrees.
…Uncover and pour barbecue
sauce over meat.
…Recover and bake one hour.
…Slice across the grain.
Serves 8.

PORT-CHEESE BEEF TENDERLOIN

INGREDIENTS

4 to 6 lb. beef tenderloin

2 c. port wine

1 c. chicken stock

1 c. cream (not half and half)

1/2 lb. Stilton cheese

2 Tbsp. oil

DIRECTIONS

…Heat oil in skillet.

…Brown tenderloin on all sides.

…Transfer meat to roasting
pan and bake uncovered at 450
degrees for 35 to 50 minutes.

…Deglaze skillet with port wine
and reduce to one half.

…Add chicken stock.

…Reduce to one half again.

…Slowly stir in cream.

…Cook over medium heat until
sauce thickens.

…Allow meat to rest after
baking for 30 minutes.

…Stir crumbled Stilton into
sauce and pour over sliced meat.
Serves 8.

STEAK A LA MOUTARDE

INGREDIENTS

4 beef tenderloins, 8 oz each

Salt and pepper

2 Tbsp. butter

2 Tbsp. shallots, finely chopped

2 Tbsp. brandy (or cognac)

1/4 c. chicken stock

3 Tbsp. Dijon mustard

2 Tbsp. chopped fresh parsley

DIRECTIONS

…Season beef with salt and pepper.

…Heat large skillet until very hot.

…Sear tenderloins for 4 minutes on
one side.

…Turn and cook to desired
temperature.

…Remove beef from skillet and
keep warm.

…Melt butter in pan and sauté
shallots 2 to 3 minutes.

…Add brandy and stock.

…Bring to a boil and stir in mustard.

…Pour sauce over beef and
garnish with parsley.
Serves 4.

TOURNEDOS IOWA

INGREDIENTS

2 Tbsp. butter

1/2 c. fresh mushrooms, sliced

1 Tbsp. flour

1/4 c. red wine

1/4 tsp. Worcestershire sauce

1/4 tsp. salt, dash pepper

4 filet mignons

1 large ripe tomato

DIRECTIONS

…Melt butter and sauté
mushrooms in sauce pan.

…Add flour and cook until
slightly browned.

…Stir in wine and seasonings.

…Cook until thickened.

…While this sauce is cooking,
season and grill filets to taste.

…Cut tomato into 4 slices
and grill.

…Place tomato slice on
each filet.

…Pour sauce over steak and
tomato.
Serves 4.

FIND A FAVORITE HOLIDAY ~ When I married into the Murphy family, I embraced the Irish Spirit! Irish eyes were smiling on us when our son was born on St. Patrick's Day. Irish blessings continued with the birth of our daughter on our wedding anniversary. Needless to say, we have fun celebrating the Irish spirit. St. Patrick's Day has become a day of family fun. We wear green (including green hair gel!), attend Irish activities (Blarney Breakfast, parades, parties…) and enjoy green cupcakes, Irish soda bread, Irish stew, or corned beef and cabbage. Another tradition we have started is sending our family newsletter around St. Patrick's Day instead of during the Christmas season. For our family, this switch has lessened the stress during Christmas and has given us a fun outlet to wish our friends and family well. Of course, there is some kind of "Irish" theme associated with the letter. Pick your favorite holiday, event, or date, and start your traditional letter. DORI MURPHY

GROUND BEEF

AWESOME SPAGHETTI SAUCE

INGREDIENTS
1 lb. hamburger
2 large onions
1 large can tomato juice
Three 6 oz. cans tomato paste
3 to 4 bay leaves
1 tsp. salt
1/4 tsp. red pepper
1/4 tsp. black pepper
Pinch garlic salt
4 heaping Tbsp. brown sugar

DIRECTIONS
…Brown hamburger and chopped onions together.
…Drain.
…Add all ingredients to one pot and simmer for 30 minutes.
…Remove bay leaves after 10 minutes.

BROWN AND SERVE MEAT LOAVES

INGREDIENTS

1 lb. ground beef
1 c. cheese crackers, crushed
1/4 c. ketchup
2 Tbsp. minced onion
1 Tbsp. Worcestershire sauce
1/3 c. evaporated milk
3/4 c. shredded cheddar cheese
1 package English muffins
1 tsp. salt
1/4 tsp. pepper

DIRECTIONS

…Preheat oven to 400 degrees.
…Split muffins in half.
…Combine all other ingredients
except cheese.
…Spread mixture on muffin
halves.
…Bake 15 minutes.
…Top with cheese and bake an
additional 5 minutes.
(Great finger food.)
Makes 12 loaves.

CATTLEMEN'S BEEF STROGANOFF

INGREDIENTS

1 lb. round or sirloin steak
2 Tbsp. butter
1/4 tsp. garlic salt
Two 10 oz. cans cream of mushroom
   soup
1 c. sour cream
2 Tbsp. Worcestershire sauce
One 4 oz. can sliced mushrooms,
   drained

DIRECTIONS

…Cut meat into 1 inch cubes.
…Brown cubes in butter.
…Stir in garlic salt, soup,
sour cream, mushrooms, and
Worcestershire sauce.
…Pour into 8x8 casserole dish.
…Bake uncovered at 325 degrees for
1 to 2 hours until meat is tender.
…Serve over cooked pasta.
Serves 4.

KANSAS CITY 1-2-3

INGREDIENTS

2 lbs. lean ground beef
2 cans cream of chicken soup, undiluted
1/2 c. medium cheddar cheese, grated
2 lbs. frozen shredded potatoes
Salt and pepper
Paprika for garnish

DIRECTIONS

…Fill a 9x13 casserole with meat
that has been seasoned with salt
and pepper.
…Press meat firmly onto bottom
and sides of pan.
…Pour soup in pan and spread
evenly over meat.
…Add potatoes, arranging in
uniform rows.
…Bake in 300 degree oven for one
hour until crisp on top.
…Drain off excess liquid.
…Sprinkle with cheese.
…Bake 3 to 5 additional minutes.
…Serve hot.
Serves 6.

ACTIVITIES FOR
GRANDCHILDREN ~ I find the best
activities my grandchildren and I
enjoy involve something using our
hands. Busy hands create happy
minds. I have taught the girls to
knit and I played ball with the
boys. But my favorite activity
is to spread the table with paper, crayons, paints, glue, and
scissors, and let the creation
begin. DONNA ADAMS

SON-OF-A-GUN SLOPPY JOES

INGREDIENTS
7 1/2 lbs. hamburger
1 large onion, chopped
4 c. celery, chopped
5 c. ketchup
1 c. water
1/8 c. lemon juice
1/2 c. vinegar
1 c. brown sugar

DIRECTIONS
…Brown hamburger.
…Drain.
…Add onion, celery, ketchup,
water, lemon juice, vinegar, and
brown sugar.
…Simmer for one hour.
Serves 36 sandwiches.

TOTO'S STROGANOFF FOR KIDS

INGREDIENTS
1 lb. ground chuck
1 large onion, chopped
1 can cream of mushroom soup
8 oz. sour cream
2 Tbsp. ketchup
1 package wide egg noodles
1 can cream of celery soup

DIRECTIONS
…Fry beef and onions until meat is
browned and onions are tender.
…Drain.
…Add mushroom soup, celery soup
and ketchup.
…Bring to a boil.
…Reduce heat and add sour cream.
…Serve over cooked egg noodles.
(Great recipe to make with your
children.)
Serves 4.

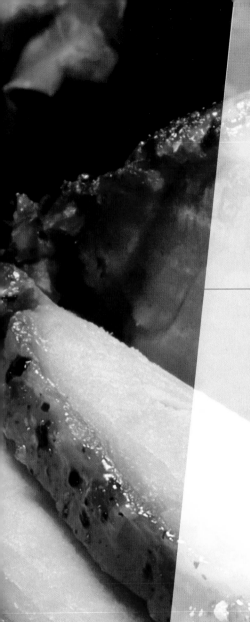

PORK

AUNT IDA'S HAM LOAF

INGREDIENTS

1 lb. ground ham
1 lb. ground beef
1 egg
1/2 c. milk
1/2 c. breadcrumbs
1 Tbsp. Worcestershire sauce
1/4 c. ketchup
Mustard
1 small can crushed pineapple
Brown sugar

DIRECTIONS

…Combine meats, egg, milk, bread-
crumbs, Worcestershire sauce, and
ketchup.
…Pat mixture in a 9 inch square pan.
…Spread layer of mustard on top.
…Top with crushed pineapple and
sprinkle with brown sugar.
…Bake one hour at 350 degrees.
Serves 6.

BOURBON PORK TENDERLOIN

INGREDIENTS

1/3 c. Worcestershire sauce
1/3 c. bourbon
1/3 c. soy sauce
One 2 lb. pork tenderloin

DIRECTIONS

…Combine Worcestershire sauce,
bourbon, and soy sauce.
…Marinate meat covered overnight.
…Place meat and marinade in
roasting pan.
…Roast meat at 350 degrees for 30
to 40 minutes.
…Baste occasionally.
…Slice tenderloin and serve hot with
marinade drizzled over the top.
Serves 4.

COWBOY PORK CHOPS AND STUFFING

INGREDIENTS
8 pork chops, thick cut
3 c. bread crumbs
2 Tbsp. chopped onion
1/4 tsp. poultry seasoning
1/4 c. melted butter
1/4 c. water
1/4 c. white wine
Oil to brown chops
Two 10 oz. cans cream of
  mushroom soup
1 c. water

DIRECTIONS
…Combine bread crumbs, onion, poultry seasoning, butter, and 1/4 c. water.
…Set aside.
…Brown chops in hot oil.
…Season.
…Slice in half to the bone.
…Stuff each chop with a mound of stuffing.
…Secure with toothpicks.
…Blend soup, 1 c. water, and wine.
…Pour over chops.
…Bake uncovered at 350 degrees for one hour.
…Serve with wild rice.
Serves 8.

MADE-IN-THE-SHADE PORK CHOPS

INGREDIENTS
4 pork chops, 1 1/4 inch thick
Two 6 oz. cans frozen lemonade
  concentrate, thawed
2/3 c. soy sauce
2 tsp. seasoned salt
1/4 tsp. garlic powder
1 tsp. celery salt

DIRECTIONS
…Mix lemonade, soy sauce, salt, garlic powder, and celery salt.
…Pour marinade over pork chops.
…Place in refrigerator for 24 hours.
…Turn meat once or twice to coat.
…Remove from refrigerator 3 to 4 hours before grilling.
…Grill over medium hot coals and baste occasionally with remaining marinade.
Serves 4.

MEXICAN PORK CHOPS

INGREDIENTS

6 large pork chops
One 15 oz. can chopped tomatoes
One 4 oz. can diced green chilies
1 c. shredded Monterey Jack cheese

DIRECTIONS

...Brown chops.
...Pour tomatoes and chilies on top.
...Cover and cook on low heat for
30 to 40 minutes or until meat is
tender.
...Spread shredded cheese on the
chops then cover and simmer until
cheese is melted.
(Serve with any pasta.)
Serves 6.

PORK TENDERLOIN WITH PINEAPPLE SALSA

INGREDIENTS

4 to 6 lbs. pork tenderloin
1 1/2 c. soy sauce
1 1/2 c. dry sherry or orange juice
3 tsp. ground ginger
6 cloves garlic, pressed

DIRECTIONS

...Mix soy sauce, sherry or orange
juice, ginger, and pressed garlic.
...Pour over the tenderloin and
marinate for 6 to 24 hours.
...Grill to desired temperature.
...Serve with pineapple salsa.
 Serves 8.

PINEAPPLE SALSA

INGREDIENTS

2 c. fresh pineapple, chopped
  (or one 20 oz. can crushed
  pineapple)
1 Tbsp. chopped cilantro
2 tsp. ginger root, minced or
  grated
1 green onion, thinly sliced
1/2 c. red pepper, chopped
1 1/2 tsp. sugar
1/2 tsp. salt
1/4 tsp. pepper

DIRECTIONS

...Mix the pineapple,
cilantro, ginger root, green
onion, red pepper, sugar, salt,
and pepper.
...Serve over the pork
tenderloin.

I HAVE FOUR CHILDREN RANGING IN AGE FROM 9 TO 19. The way I coax my children to clean their rooms is to enforce the requirement that before they can do anything on the weekend, they must have their rooms picked up and clean by Friday night. It certainly makes the weekend less stressful when you walk by tidy bedrooms! Nothing motivates a child faster than missing out on fun, whether it's with family or friends. And believe me, it only takes one time of standing firm to have your home running smoother.

RENE SMITH

VENISON & LAMB

CHUCK WAGON VENISON STROGANOFF

INGREDIENTS
1 clove garlic, minced
1/2 c. chopped onion
2 Tbsp. oil
1 lb. venison, cut in
   2 inch strips
1/4 c. flour
1/2 tsp. salt
1/8 tsp. pepper
One 3 oz. can sliced
   mushrooms
1/2 c. beef bouillon
1/2 c. sour cream

DIRECTIONS
…Sauté onion and garlic in oil.
…Dredge venison in flour seasoned with salt and pepper.
…Brown in onion mixture.
…Add undrained mushrooms and beef bouillon.
…Cover and cook over low heat for one hour.
…Add sour cream during the last 15 minutes.
…Serve over noodles or rice.
(Dish is low in fat. This recipe takes the "gamey" taste out of the venison and provides a very tender, healthy alternative to beef.)
Serves 2 to 4.

FLINT HILLS LEG OF LAMB

INGREDIENTS
8 to 9 lb. leg of lamb (boned and rolled if desired)
Cooking oil
1 to 2 cloves garlic
1 tsp. seasoned salt
1 tsp. salt
Cracked black pepper
1/2 tsp. thyme
Steak seasoning

DIRECTIONS
…Rub lamb with clove of garlic.
…Rub lightly with oil.
…Combine seasonings, thyme, and salt, and rub over surface.
…Place on rack in a shallow roasting pan, fat side up.
…Sprinkle generously with cracked black pepper to cover entire surface and press in lightly.
…Roast in preheated 325 degree oven,
…(Insert meat thermometer into thickest part of meat so that it does not touch the bone.)
…Internal temperature should be 175 to 182 degrees, depending on desired doneness.
…This will take 3 to 4 hours.
…Lamb should be served hot or cold, never warm.
…Remove to hot platter, cover with foil. Serve within 15 minutes.
…Serve with potatoes and horseradish mustard.
Note: 5 to 6 pound leg of lamb will take 2 1/2 to 3 hours.
Serves 8 to 10.

VEAL MARSALA

INGREDIENTS
6 veal cutlets
1/4 c. flour
1/4 c. minced shallots
1 clove garlic, minced
1/2 lb. sliced mushrooms
1/2 c. Marsala wine

DIRECTIONS
…Pound veal with a mallet between sheets of wax paper until thin.
…Dredge meat in flour.
…In skillet, sauté shallots, mushrooms, and garlic.
…Remove from pan.
…Add veal and sauté on each side until golden.
…Add wine and vegetables and cook until tender.
…Serve with rice or pasta.
(May also be made with chicken.)
Serves 6.

CHICKEN GAME & FISH CHICKEN GAME & FISH CHICKEN GAME & FISH CHICKEN GAME & FISH CHI

Chicken, Game, & Fish

CHICKEN

CHICKEN A LA CAN-CAN

INGREDIENTS
1 can (10 1/2 oz.) cream of chicken soup
1 can (10 1/2 oz.) cream of celery soup
1 soup can of water
1 can (12 oz.) boned chicken or 1 1/2 c.
  cooked chicken pieces
1 soup can (1 1/3 c.) minute rice
1 can (3 1/2 oz.) French fried onions.

DIRECTIONS
...Combine soups, water, and chicken.
...Add minute rice, uncooked.
...Mix.
...Simmer on top of the stove for 7 minutes.
...Top with French fried onions.
Serves 6.

CHICKEN BREASTS IN LEMON CREAM SAUCE

INGREDIENTS
6 chicken breasts, skinned
 and flattened
1 stick butter
1/4 c. sherry
4 tsp. grated lemon peel
1/4 c. lemon juice
2 c. cream
Salt, pepper, paprika

DIRECTIONS
...Split breasts, dry well, and season
with salt, pepper, and paprika.
...Sauté chicken in butter until
browned, 5 to 8 minutes.
...Place chicken on oven safe
serving platter and place in a
warm oven.
...To the sauté pan add sherry,
lemon peel, and lemon juice. Cook
for 1 minute.
...Allow pan to cool slightly and add
cream slowly.
...Heat.
...Spoon over the chicken and serve.
Serves 6.

CHICKEN PARMIGIANA

INGREDIENTS

4 chicken breasts, skinless and boneless
1 egg, slightly beaten
1 c. seasoned bread crumbs
1/4 c. butter
One 14 oz. jar chunky spaghetti sauce
One 8 oz. package mozzarella cheese, shredded
Grated Parmesan cheese

DIRECTIONS

…Preheat oven to 350 degrees.
…Dip chicken breast into egg.
…Coat with bread crumbs.
…Heat butter in skillet and brown chicken on both sides.
…Pour a layer of spaghetti sauce onto bottom of 9x13 casserole dish.
…Arrange chicken in layer over sauce.
…Sprinkle shredded mozzarella cheese over chicken.
…Pour remaining sauce over cheese and cover.
…Sprinkle with Parmesan cheese and bake 30 minutes.
…Serve with spaghetti, salad, and bread sticks.
Serves 4.

CHIPOTLE MARINATED CHICKEN

INGREDIENTS

6 boneless, skinless chicken breasts
1 chipotle pepper seeded and steeped for 10 minutes
2 oz. sun dried cherries
2 oz. sun dried cranberries
2 oz. brandy or other fortified wine
Salt and pepper to taste
4 oz. oil
4 oz. chicken stock
1 Tbsp. corn starch
2 Tbsp. cool water
Zest of 1 orange

DIRECTIONS

…Once you have steeped the pepper, place in a blender with oil and blend until smooth.
…Pour over chicken and let marinate for one hour.
…Place cherries and cranberries in brandy and let them soak for 20 minutes or longer.
…Combine water and cornstarch. (It should resemble the consistency of milk.)
…Simmer chicken stock, cherries, cranberries, and brandy.
…Add orange zest.
…Thicken with cornstarch mixture until it coats the back of a spoon.
…Do not overcook. (It should be clear.)
…Keep warm.
…Grill chicken.
…Pour sauce over grilled chicken.
…Serve with your favorite vegetable and starch.
Serves 6.

DUTCH OVEN CHICKEN

INGREDIENTS

6 chicken breasts,
   skinned and boned
2 Tbsp. butter
2 Tbsp. olive oil
1 c. chopped onion
2 Tbsp. paprika
1 tsp. salt
2 c. chicken stock
1 c. sour cream
One 4 oz. can
   chopped tomatoes

DIRECTIONS

…Simmer chopped onion in butter and olive oil until soft.
…Add paprika and cook until golden.
…Add salt and chicken stock and bring to a boil.
…Cut chicken breasts into 2 to 3 inch strips.
…Add chicken and tomatoes to sauce.
…Simmer until chicken is tender, about 1 hour.
…Stir in sour cream and heat thoroughly.
…Do not boil.
…Serve over rice or pasta. Serves 6.

WORKING MOTHERHOOD ~ Being a working mother of four active children does not seem unusual to me, because I decided early on that I wanted it all: to practice law and raise a family. How do I manage? Some areas of my life do not get as much attention as others. For example, dust bunnies do exist and cohabitate peacefully alongside my family. But since I do work long hours, our family makes it a point to eat dinner together. (Absolutely no TV.) My children call it our 1950's sitcom moment: mother cooking dinner and everyone sitting down to eat together. It is our time to catch up with each other's lives. I do not regard the time spent cooking as cooking, per se, it is more meal preparation. CAROL B. BONEBRAKE

HEN HOUSE CHICKEN

INGREDIENTS

4 chicken breasts, boneless and
  skinless
1/2 c. low fat ranch dressing
1 c. Melba toast crumbs
1/2 c. Parmesan cheese
Salt and pepper

DIRECTIONS

…Mix ranch dressing with 2 Tbsp.
water in a large flat bowl.
…Mix 1 c. Melba toast crumbs with
1/2 c. Parmesan cheese in a second
large flat bowl.
…Salt and pepper chicken.
…Dip chicken first in the ranch
dressing and then into the crumb
mixture.
…Bake in oven at 350 degrees for 35
minutes.
(You may substitute bread crumbs or
Rice Krispy crumbs for Melba toast
crumbs.)
Serves 4.

LIME SALSA GRILLED CHICKEN

INGREDIENTS

8 chicken breasts
Juice of 2 fresh limes
1/2 c. olive oil
1 c. salsa
2 to 4 tsp. chili powder

DIRECTIONS

…Combine lime juice (reserving
1 tsp. juice) and olive oil in a
Ziplock bag.
…Add chicken, seal, and
marinate for 1 to 2 hours.
…Combine salsa, 1 tsp. lime
juice, and chili powder.
…Remove chicken from
marinade and place on hot grill.
…Cook until done, basting with
salsa mixture when turning.
Serves 8.

NO-RECIPE PARTY PARMESAN CHICKEN

INGREDIENTS

8 boned chicken breasts
1 pkg. (4 oz.) saltine crackers,
  crushed
Parmesan cheese
1 c. butter or margarine,
  melted

DIRECTIONS

…Place chicken on the bottom of
a 9x13 inch casserole dish.
…Sprinkle saltine crackers on
top.
…Sprinkle with cheese and
drizzle butter over the top.
…Bake at 325 degrees for 25 to
30 minutes.
(Don't over bake.)
Serves 8.

PIONEER CHICKEN

INGREDIENTS
1 chicken, cut into parts
1/2 c. onion
2 Tbsp. butter
1/2 c. celery, chopped
1/4 c. green pepper, chopped
1 c. ketchup
2 Tbsp. Worcestershire sauce
2 Tbsp. brown sugar
Pepper to taste

DIRECTIONS
…Brown chicken pieces in oil and place in a casserole dish.
…Sauté onion in butter.
…Add celery, green pepper, ketchup, water, Worcestershire sauce and brown sugar.
…Bring to a boil.
…Pour over chicken.
…Cover and bake at 350 degrees for one hour.
(May be made ahead. It's even better warmed over the next day.)
(For a thicker sauce, remove lid during last 15 minutes of baking time.)
Serves 4.

POPPY SEED CHICKEN

INGREDIENTS
1 chicken cooked and boned
  (or 4 chicken breasts, cooked and diced)
1 can cream of chicken soup
1 can cream of celery soup
One 8 oz. carton sour cream
One 4 oz. package sliced almonds
1 c. Minute Rice, cooked
1 roll Ritz crackers
1 stick margarine
3 Tbsp. poppy seeds

DIRECTIONS
…Mix chicken, soups, sour cream, almonds, and rice and pour into 9x13 casserole dish.
…Crush crackers and mix with melted margarine.
…Sprinkle over casserole.
…Sprinkle top with poppy seeds.
…Bake at 350 degrees for 30 minutes.
Serves 4.

SUNDAY CHICKEN WELLINGTON

INGREDIENTS

4 large chicken breasts,
  skinned and boned
8 oz. package cream cheese,
  softened
One 4 oz. can mushrooms,
  drained
1 Tbsp. chopped green onion
1/4 tsp. salt
1/4 tsp. pepper
One 10 oz. can refrigerated
  crescent rolls
1 egg, slightly beaten

Sauce
3 Tbsp. butter
1 Tbsp. green onion, chopped
2 1/2 Tbsp. flour
1 1/4 c. evaporated milk
1/4 c. white wine
1/2 tsp. salt
One 2 oz. can mushrooms,
  drained

DIRECTIONS

…Place chicken breasts between 2 pieces of plastic wrap and roll to 1/8 inch thickness.
…Combine cream cheese, mushrooms, onion, salt, and pepper.
…Place 2 Tbsp. of the mixture in the center of each chicken piece.
…Start with the small end, roll up and secure with toothpicks.
…Melt butter in skillet.
…Sauté chicken rolls, turning occasionally, 6 minutes or until opaque.
…Set aside.
…Separate dough into 4 triangles.
…Seal perforations and roll into 6x7 inch rectangles.
…Remove toothpicks from chicken and place in center of dough.
…Wrap around chicken and seal edges.
…Place seam side down on ungreased cookie sheet.
…Brush with egg.
…Bake 18 to 20 minutes at 375 degrees.
…For sauce, melt butter and sauté onion until tender.
…Blend in flour.
…Gradually add milk.
…Stir in wine and cook until thickened.
…Add salt and mushrooms.
…Serve over chicken rolls.
Serves 4.

SUNFLOWER CHICKEN

INGREDIENTS

6 boneless chicken breasts
6 slices Swiss cheese
1 can cream of chicken soup
1/4 c. white wine
2 c. stuffing mix
1/3 c. butter, melted

DIRECTIONS

…Place chicken in 9x13 pan.
…Place Swiss cheese over chicken.
…Mix wine and soup.
…Pour over chicken.
…Sprinkle stuffing mix on top.
…Drizzle melted butter over top.
…Bake at 350 degrees for 50 minutes.
Serves 6.

TUSCAN CHICKEN

INGREDIENTS

1 lb. chicken breast cut into
* 1 inch cubes*
2 cloves garlic, minced
2 Tbsp. oil
4 potatoes, cut into cubes
1 medium red pepper, diced
One 27 oz. jar spaghetti sauce
1 lb. fresh or frozen green beans
1 tsp. dried basil
Salt and pepper to taste

DIRECTIONS

…Sauté chicken and garlic in oil until lightly brown.
…Add potatoes and pepper.
…Cook for 5 minutes.
…Add the spaghetti sauce, basil, green beans, salt and pepper.
…Bring to a boil.
…Reduce heat to simmer and cook for a half hour, covered or until the chicken is cooked and potatoes are tender. Stir occasionally.
Serves 4 to 6.

THE BRIDE'S WAY ~ Our daughter is getting married, and the best advice I've received is that when there is a disagreement between the bride and her mother, the <u>bride</u> makes the decision. ANONYMOUS

THEIR OWN PATH ~ When talking with my children about their future lives, I felt this saying was most meaningful: "Do not follow where the path may lead. Go instead where there is no path and leave a trail."
SARAH BAILEY

GAME

SAVORY QUAIL BREASTS

INGREDIENTS
2 to 3 breasts per person
1 lb. bacon
Lemon butter

DIRECTIONS
…Wrap breasts in bacon.
…Secure with toothpicks.
…Broil 6 to 8 inches from broiler.
…Allow 8 minutes per side.
…You may serve breasts on the platter as is or remove the bacon.
…A sauce of 1/2 lemon juice and 1/2 butter makes a good dipping sauce.

SETTLER'S CREAMED PHEASANT

INGREDIENTS
1 whole pheasant
1 pint cream
1 can cream of mushroom soup
1 large onion
1 c. carrots, sliced
2 c. cubed potatoes
Oil

DIRECTIONS
…Sear cut up pheasant in roasting pan.
…Mix soup, cream, and onions. Pour over pheasant.
…Bake at 300 degrees until meat is very tender.
(For variety you may add potatoes and carrots to the meat the last hour in the oven.)
Serves 4.

FISH

AUNT MAE'S SALMON PATTIES

INGREDIENTS
2 cans salmon
3 eggs, beaten
1/2 c. milk
1/2 tsp. salt
2 dashes Tabasco
1 tsp. seafood seasoning
1 c. finely crushed cracker crumbs
1 medium onion, minced
Dill (optional)

DIRECTIONS
…Remove dark skin and bones from salmon.
…Drain salmon but do not rinse.
…Mix salmon gently with other ingredients and form into patties.
…Cook quickly in a hot skillet with a small amount of oil and butter.
…Serve with Hollandaise sauce.
…Sprinkle with dill.
Serves 4.

BROILED SCALLOPS

INGREDIENTS
1/2 c. butter
1 clove garlic, minced
2 lb. bay scallops
1/4 c. flour
1 tsp. paprika
White pepper to taste
Cayenne pepper to taste

DIRECTIONS
…Melt butter and garlic.
…Pour half of the butter into shallow baking dish in single layer.
…Layer on scallops.
…Combine flour, paprika, pepper, and cayenne.
…Sprinkle over scallops.
…Pour remaining butter on top.
…Broil scallops until brown, 6 to 8 minutes.
Serves 4.

DEVILED OYSTERS

INGREDIENTS

1 pt. fresh oysters, including liquid
1/4 c. butter, melted
1 c. oyster cracker crumbs
1 medium green pepper, seeded and
  chopped
1/4 c. parsley, finely chopped
1 medium onion, grated
2 tsp. Worcestershire sauce
2 boiled eggs, chopped
3 eggs, lightly beaten
1/4 c. light cream
1/4 tsp. dry mustard
Cayenne pepper and salt to taste

DIRECTIONS

...Preheat oven to 375 degrees.
...Combine all ingredients and mix well.
...Pour into 2 qt. soufflé or casserole
dish.
...Bake 30 minutes until set and lightly
browned.
Serves 4.

GRILLED SHRIMP PACKAGES

INGREDIENTS

1 lb. large fresh raw
  shrimp
Extra virgin olive oil
Fresh herbs of choice
Salt and fresh ground
  pepper
Garlic cloves
Tin foil squares

DIRECTIONS

...Rinse and devein approx. 4 to 5 large
shrimp per person.
...Set aside while you cut tin foil into 8
to 10 inch squares.
...Place 4 to 5 shrimp in the middle of
each foil square.
...Drizzle a tsp. of olive oil on each
shrimp group.
...Sprinkle a pinch of fresh thyme,
summer savory, (lemon verbena, chives,
rosemary) or other combination of herbs.
...Finish with a dash of sea salt and
fresh ground pepper accompanied by
sliced clove of garlic.
...Gather corners of tinfoil squares
above center.
...Crimp edges together to make "tent"
for shrimp to steam.
...Place tin foil packages right on the
grill with the rest of the meal.
...Takes about 6 to 8 minutes.
Serves 4.

JOSEPHINE'S LOBSTER AU GRATIN

INGREDIENTS
4 Tbsp. butter
2 Tbsp. flour
1/2 tsp. dry mustard
1 1/2 c. light cream
3 Tbsp. Parmesan cheese
1 egg yolk, beaten
1 lb. lobster, cut up
1/2 c. sliced mushrooms
2 Tbsp. sherry (optional)
Salt to taste

DIRECTIONS
…Melt butter and gradually add flour and mustard.
…Add cream.
…Cook over low heat, stirring constantly until thickened.
…Blend in 2 Tbsp. cheese and salt.
…Mix a little sauce into egg yolk, then stir yolk quickly into sauce.
…Stir in 1 Tbsp. butter.
…Add lobster, mushrooms, and sherry.
…Spoon into casserole.
…Dot with remaining 1 Tbsp. butter.
…Bake at 400 degrees until browned, about 15 minutes.
Serves 2 to 4.

NEOSHO RIVER FRIED CATFISH

INGREDIENTS
4 catfish filets
1 c. yellow corn meal
1/2 tsp. marjoram
1/2 tsp. thyme
1 Tbsp. salt
1/4 tsp. pepper

DIRECTIONS
…Combine the corn meal, marjoram, thyme, salt, and pepper in a bowl.
…Dredge the catfish in the corn meal.
…Fry in hot oil until the fish is golden brown and flakes easily with a fork.
Serves 4.

CHOOSE YOUR BATTLES ~ When I was a younger mother, I had the foolish idea that a teenager's room should be neat all the time. I soon had to surrender this idea with our son, but I had high hopes for his younger sister. She was very active in extra-curricular activities. One day, when I was telling her to clean her room, she said, "Do you want me in all these activities, or do you want this bed made?" I realized that no college application ever asks if the student is neat. So, reluctantly, I let that one go, and instead just kept her door shut. She was accepted by her college of choice, and when she moved in with her college roommates, she became a much neater person. LINDA POLLY

COOKING UP CONVERSATIONS ~ We liked to have our children give parties and overnights for their friends in our house so we would know where they were. It also was a good way for me to learn what was going on. For each party, I would make homemade cinnamon rolls and chocolate chip cookies. My trick was to purposely let the dough rise as long as necessary so I would be baking the bread while their friends were in the house. Of course, they smelled the cinnamon rolls in the oven and migrated to the kitchen to wait until they were frosted and the cookies came out of the other oven. If I kept quiet, they would talk to each other. In this way, I learned what was going on with all the kids in school. LINDA POLLY

ORANGE ROUGHY PARMESAN

INGREDIENTS
2 lb. orange roughy filets
2 Tbsp. fresh lemon juice
1/2 c. Parmesan cheese
1/4 c. butter, softened
3 Tbsp. mayonnaise
3 Tbsp. chopped green onions
1/4 tsp. salt
Dash Tabasco sauce
Pepper to taste

DIRECTIONS
…In a buttered casserole, place filets in a single layer.
…Brush with lemon juice.
…Let stand 10 minutes.
…In a small bowl, combine cheese, butter, mayonnaise, onions, salt, pepper, and Tabasco sauce.
…Broil filets 3 to 4 inches under broiler for 5 minutes.
…Spread with cheese mixture for an additional 2 to 3 minutes.
…Watch closely so filets do not burn.
Serves 6.

SHRIMP A LA GARDEN

INGREDIENTS
1 lb. large shrimp, cooked and peeled
1 lb. fresh pea pods
One 16 oz. bottle zesty Italian salad dressing
1/4 c. fresh chopped parsley
1/2 tsp. garlic salt
1/4 tsp. pepper

DIRECTIONS
…Wrap each shrimp in a pea pod.
…Secure with a toothpick.
…Place all in a glass bowl.
…Add salad dressing, parsley, garlic salt, and pepper.
…Toss gently and chill covered.
(A great party hors d'oeuvre.)

SHRIMP CREOLE

INGREDIENTS
2 c. cooked shrimp
2 Tbsp. butter, melted
1 c. onion, chopped
1 c. bell pepper, chopped
1/2 tsp. garlic salt
1 can chopped tomatoes

DIRECTIONS
...Melt butter.
...Add onion, pepper, and garlic salt.
...Cook until tender.
...Add tomatoes, salt, and pepper.
...Bring to a boil.
...Add shrimp and heat.
...Serve over rice.
Serves 6.

SHRIMP DE JONGHE

INGREDIENTS
2 lb. shrimp, cooked and cleaned
1 c. butter, melted
2 cloves garlic, minced
1/3 c. parsley, chopped fresh
1/2 c. cooking sherry
2 c. soft bread crumbs

DIRECTIONS
...Add butter, garlic, parsley, paprika, and sherry to shrimp.
...Mix.
...Add bread crumbs.
...Toss.
...Place shrimp into greased casserole dish.
...Bake at 350 degrees until top is brown and shrimp is hot.
Serves 4.

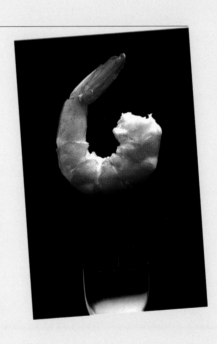

Vegetables & side dishes

ISHES VEGETABLES & SIDE DISHES VEGETABLES & SIDE DISHES VEGETABLES & SIDE DISHES VEGETABLES & SIDE DISHES VEGETABLES & SIDE DISHES VEGETABLES & SIDE DISHES VEGETABLES & SIDE DISHES VEGETABLES & SIDE DISHES VEGETABLES

ARTICHOKE-RICE SALAD

INGREDIENTS
1 package chicken flavored rice mix
4 green onions, thinly sliced
1 green pepper, chopped
12 pimiento-stuffed olives, sliced
Two 6 oz. jars marinated artichoke
  hearts
1/3 c. mayonnaise
3/4 tsp. curry powder

DIRECTIONS
…Cook rice as directed on package.
…Cool in large bowl.
…Add onion, pepper, and olives.
…Drain artichokes, reserving
marinade.
…Combine mayonnaise, curry
powder, and half of marinade.
…Add sauce and artichoke hearts
to rice mixture and toss.
…Chill several hours or overnight.
Serves 8.

AUNT JANE'S GREEN BEANS

INGREDIENTS
1 1/2 lb. green beans, trimmed
6 Tbsp. butter
2 Tbsp. lemon juice
1 1/2 tsp. dried dill
1/2 clove garlic, crushed
1 Tbsp. chopped parsley
10 cherry tomatoes, halved
1/2 c. ripe olives, sliced
Salt and pepper

DIRECTIONS
…Cook beans in salted water
until tender.
…Drain.
…Melt butter in pan.
…Add beans, lemon juice, dill,
garlic, and parsley.
…Toss.
…Add tomatoes and olives.
…Serve warm.
…Season with salt and pepper.
Serves 8.

AUTUMN MARMALADE CARROTS

INGREDIENTS
2 lbs. carrots, julienned
6 Tbsp. orange juice
1/4 c. maple syrup
2 Tbsp. orange marmalade

DIRECTIONS
…Steam carrots until tender.
…Set aside.
…In another pan combine orange
juice, maple syrup, and marmalade.
…Bring to a boil, stirring constantly.
…Add carrots and stir to coat.
…Reduce heat and simmer for 3
minutes.
Serves 6 to 8.

DISTRACT TANTRUMS ~ Children throw tantrums. I found that it is better to avoid a confrontation, a "war of wills," by distracting them: either by making a joke or pointing out something that will distract them. This gives them an opportunity to get themselves under control. Children don't want to be angry any more than we want them to be angry. Once I took a temper-tantrum out of the house, into the car, and for a drive to a pond nearby to feed the ducks. My child calmed down immediately and a very nice conversation ensued. Children appreciate your help in letting them gain self-control. BETH TRIMBLE BURNETT

BACON AND ASPARAGUS FRITTATA

INGREDIENTS

1 lb. bacon
1 c. fresh or frozen asparagus
  (cut into 1/2 inch lengths)
1 c. chopped onion
2 cloves garlic, minced
10 large eggs
1/4 c. parsley, minced
1/4 tsp. seasoned salt
1/4 tsp. fresh ground pepper
1 tomato, thinly sliced
1/4 c. grated cheddar
  cheese

DIRECTIONS

...Cook bacon and drain.
...Save 1 Tbsp. bacon drippings.
...Heat bacon drippings in 9 inch or
10 inch oven-proof skillet.
...Add asparagus, onion, and garlic.
...Sauté until onion is soft.
...Crumble bacon.
...Save 1/3 of the bacon.
...Sprinkle 2/3 of bacon over
vegetables.
...In a large bowl beat eggs,
parsley, salt, and pepper.
...Pour egg mixture into skillet.
...Arrange tomato slices on top.
...Sprinkle with cheese and
remaining 1/3 bacon.
...Cover and cook over low heat
10 to 15 minutes or until eggs are
nearly set.
...Broil 6 inches from broiler for 2
minutes or until lightly browned.
Serves 8.

BAKED PINEAPPLE STUFFING

INGREDIENTS
1/4 c. butter
1 c. sugar
4 eggs
One 20 oz. can crushed pineapple, drained
6 slices French bread, cubed

DIRECTIONS
…Beat butter, sugar, and eggs until fluffy.
…Pour over pineapple and bread cubes and stir well.
…Pour into flat casserole.
…Bake at 350 degrees for 45 minutes or until edges and top begin to brown.
Serves 6.

BAKED RUM SWEET POTATOES

INGREDIENTS
6 large sweet potatoes
1/2 tsp. salt
1 tsp. pumpkin pie spice
1/4 c. brown sugar
1/2 c. butter
1/2 c. evaporated milk
2 eggs, beaten
1/2 c. chopped pecans
1 jigger (1 1/2 oz.) rum
3/4 c. miniature marshmallows

DIRECTIONS
…Boil sweet potatoes with salt until soft, drain then mash.
…Add all other ingredients except marshmallows.
…Pour into buttered 9x13 pan.
…Top with marshmallows.
…Bake at 350 degrees for 15 to 30 minutes.
Serves 8.

BASIC PASTA

INGREDIENTS
6 eggs
Flour
2 Tbsp. fresh parsley
1 Tbsp. dill
Garlic salt
Pepper

DIRECTIONS
…Put eggs in a food processor.
…Add seasonings.
…Add as much flour as you can in the food processor.
…Blend.
…Turn pasta out onto the counter.
…Knead in flour until the noodles can be rolled and cut (or put through pasta machine).
…Dry before boiling.
Serves 8.

PASTA VARIATIONS
Tomato Pasta: Add 1/4 c. tomato paste to egg mixture. Spinach Pasta: Add 1/2 c. finely pureed spinach to egg mixture. Whole Wheat Pasta: Substitute 1/2 whole wheat flour for 1/2 of the white flour in the recipe.

BASIL-TOMATO PASTA

INGREDIENTS
10 tomatoes, chopped
1/2 c. basil leaves, chopped
2 onions, finely chopped
8 cloves garlic, minced
2 Tbsp. olive oil
2 Tbsp. parsley, chopped
10 oz. bow tie pasta

DIRECTIONS
…Sauté onion in oil until translucent.
…Add garlic.
…Add salt, tomatoes, basil, and parsley.
…Sauté for 30 minutes.
…Boil bow tie pasta. Drain.
…Pour onto serving dish.
…Pour tomato-basil sauce on top.
Serves 8.

CELERY CASSEROLE

INGREDIENTS
2 c. celery, cut into bite-sized
  pieces
10 3/4 oz. can cream of chicken soup
1/3 c. slivered almonds
Grated cheddar cheese
Bread crumbs
Butter

DIRECTIONS
…Steam celery until crisp and bright green.
…Drain.
…Mix in soup and almonds.
…Place in shallow casserole.
…Cover with grated cheese and bread crumbs. Dot with butter.
…Bake at 375 degrees for 30 minutes.
Serves 4 to 6.

COUNTRY BAKED BEANS

INGREDIENTS
Two 16 oz. cans pork and beans
3/4 c. BBQ sauce
1/2 c. brown sugar
1 tart apple, cored, peeled, and
  chopped
1/2 small onion, chopped
2 Tbsp. golden raisins
3 strips bacon

DIRECTIONS
…Brown and drain bacon.
…Mix bacon and all other ingredients and place in a large casserole.
…Bake at 350 degrees for one hour.
Serves 6 to 8.

CHOOSING COLLEGES ~

Trying to be good parents, we let our daughter enroll in the university of her dreams half-way across the country. Everything would be perfect she told us. Unfortunately, reality set in after the first semester and the dream became a nightmare. The housing situation was so terrible she was unable to study effectively. She is now back home in one of our state's universities and much happier. But we learned a few things that we should have done to help her avoid this major trauma. First, check out what the dorms for first year students are really like. During our trip they showed us the model dorms, but didn't tell us only juniors and seniors could live in them. Second, speak with the Resident Advisors (RA). To a large extent, they determine the quality of life and the conduct of the other students in the dormitories. Third, speak to students who have graduated from the university and ask them about the living conditions and quality of education. Fourth, look at the neighborhood crime rate. Our daughter's dorm was in a bad section of the city, which made her feel unsafe at night. Hopefully, these tips will help your family avoid the mistakes we made.

JANE HANSEN

DUMPLINGS

INGREDIENTS
2 c. Bisquick
2/3 c. milk

DIRECTIONS
…Mix the 2 ingredients until soft dough forms.
…Drop by spoonfuls onto boiling stew or chicken.
…Reduce heat and cook uncovered for 10 minutes.
…Cover and cook an additional 10 minutes.

EGGPLANT PARMIGIANA

INGREDIENTS
1 eggplant
4 eggs, beaten
Flour
Bread crumbs
1 jar spaghetti sauce
One 8 oz. package
  mozzarella cheese
Salt
Oregano
Basil

DIRECTIONS
...Slice eggplant and place on a
platter.
...Salt.
...Let juices run out for one hour.
...Fill one soup bowl with flour, one
bowl with 4 beaten eggs, and one
bowl with bread crumbs.
...Dip slices in flour, eggs, and
bread crumbs.
...Lightly fry in oil.
...Drain.
...Place in casserole dish.
...Layer with spaghetti sauce, then
thinly sliced mozzarella.
...Repeat layers.
...Top with oregano and basil.
...Bake for 25 minutes at 350 degrees.
...Cover with foil the last 10 to 15
minutes.
...Top layer of cheese should be
lightly browned.
Serves 6 to 8.

FEED STORE CORN WITH CILANTRO

INGREDIENTS
8 ears of corn (remove from
  the cob uncooked)
2 Tbsp. olive oil
4 Tbsp. green onion
1 chopped red pepper
1/4 tsp. cayenne pepper
1/2 c. chopped cilantro

DIRECTIONS
...Remove corn from the cob.
...In a saucepan, sauté onion in
olive oil.
...Add red pepper and corn.
...Sauté 5 minutes.
...Remove from heat and add
1/4 tsp. cayenne pepper and
cilantro.
Serves 8.

FRIED BARLEY

INGREDIENTS
1 3/4 c. barley
2 Tbsp. onion
2 cans consommé
2 cans water
1 can mushrooms

DIRECTIONS
…Mix all the ingredients and season with salt and pepper.
…Bake in greased casserole for one hour at 350 degrees.
(Good substitute for potatoes.)
Serves 4 to 6.

FRIED RICE

INGREDIENTS
1 egg, slightly beaten
2 tsp. butter
2 Tbsp. scallions, chopped
1 1/2 c. instant brown rice
1 1/2 c. chicken or beef broth

DIRECTIONS
…Cook egg slowly in butter until egg is set.
…Stir into scallions and rice until lightly browned.
…Add broth and bring to a boil.
…Cover.
…Reduce heat and let simmer 5 minutes.
Serves 4 to 6.

ROLE MODELS ~ It's never too late for role models. I've found one who is a local legend. If you live almost anywhere in our city you have heard of Dorothy Fager. She is a great grandmother and is the glue that holds this family together. Watching her has taught me the simplest things can help us connect with our offspring. She is involved in every stage of each generation of Fagers. She was the first in the door at school events, walked the grandkids on the golf course, helped them move to new homes over and over again, and is still baby sitting the great grandchildren. The family says the little ones sense her seniority, calmness, and determination. She has a snack cupboard in a lower cabinet with a handle even the smallest Fager can reach. She is a tiny little woman with a smile and a heart as big as she is. I am not a grandmother but when I am I will go to Dorothy Fager for advice. LINDA POLLY

FRIED TOMATOES

INGREDIENTS
4 firm tomatoes
Salt and Pepper
Flour
Bacon drippings

DIRECTIONS
…Wash and stem tomatoes.
…Cut into 1/2 inch slices.
…Season and dust with flour.
…Fry in bacon drippings until
crisp, turning once.
…Drain on paper towels.
Serves 4 to 6.

GARDEN GREEN BEANS AND PEA PODS

INGREDIENTS
5 slices bacon, chopped
1 small onion, sliced
1 lb. fresh green beans, broken
  into pieces
1/4 lb. fresh pea pods
1 tsp. sugar
1/2 tsp. salt

DIRECTIONS
…Fry bacon and add onion,
cooking until translucent.
…Add beans and pea pods.
…Stir-fry until bright green.
…Add 1/4 c. water.
…Simmer covered no longer
than 4 minutes.
…Add sugar and salt.
…Serve immediately.
Serves 4 to 6.

GREEN CHILI CHEESE PIE

INGREDIENTS
One 4 oz. can chopped green
  chilies, drained
3/4 lb. Monterey Jack cheese,
  grated
4 eggs beaten
Salt and white pepper to taste

DIRECTIONS
…Beat eggs well.
…Add cheese, chilies, salt,
and white pepper.
…Pour into lightly buttered
8x8 pan.
…Bake at 350 degrees for 40
minutes or until golden.
…May be served hot, room
temperature, or cold.
Serves 6 to 8.

HARVEST CARROTS WITH RAISINS

INGREDIENTS
1 1/2 lb. carrots
1/4 c. butter
1/3 c. dry white wine
1/2 tsp. nutmeg
2/3 c. light raisins
3 Tbsp. brown sugar

DIRECTIONS
…Peel carrots and cut into 1/4 inch slices.
…Put into saucepan with butter, wine, and nutmeg.
…Cover and cook until tender.
…Stir in raisins and brown sugar.
…Continue cooking for a few minutes until raisins are plump and carrots glazed.
Serves 6.

HOT CURRIED FRUIT

INGREDIENTS
One 29 oz. can pear halves
One 20 oz. can chunk pineapple
One 29 oz. can peach slices
One 29 oz. can apricot halves
1/2 c. butter
1 c. brown sugar
1 Tbsp. cornstarch
1 1/2 tsp. curry powder

DIRECTIONS
…Drain all fruits well.
…Pour into 9x13 casserole.
…Make a sauce of butter, brown sugar, cornstarch, and curry powder.
…Spoon sauce over fruits.
…Bake at 325 degrees for one hour, stirring occasionally.
Serves 12.

A FEW EXTRA WINKS ~

Every mother of an infant learns how important getting enough sleep is. One of my solutions was to make a bag out of fabric scraps and tie it to the end of our daughter's bed. I filled it with soft toys and books ,which would keep her entertained for a short period of time each morning. "Soft" is the operative word. I learned this the hard way when we first introduced this idea and heard the heavy toys hitting the wall as our daughter heaved them across the room. LINDA POLLY

CHILDHOOD RELIGION ~ My parents took me to church weekly from infancy and encouraged my involvement in our church's youth group. I came in contact with many adults who helped me mature in my faith. In addition to teaching me to love the Lord, they taught me to love others. When there were life questions I felt I could not talk to my parents about, I would ask these adults. My advice is to find a place where your children have time with other adults who share your values. Your children will have questions; life is certainly full of them, and the answers they receive when they are young will significantly impact their lives. DIANA JOLIFF

JALAPEÑO CARROTS

INGREDIENTS
6 c. carrots, sliced into small strips
  (or cut at an angle)
1/2 c. butter
1/2 tsp. salt
2/3 c. jalapeño jelly
2 Tbsp. parsley, chopped

DIRECTIONS
…Place carrots and butter in saucepan.
…Cover with buttered wax paper or foil.
…Cook on low heat until carrots are tender.
(Do not add water. This is the sweating method.)
…Add salt.
…Let carrots cook additional minutes to absorb the liquid.
…Toss with jelly.
…Sprinkle with parsley.
(Delicious with ham or pork.)
Serves 6.

LEMON GLAZED CARROTS

INGREDIENTS
1 lb. carrots, peeled
2 Tbsp. butter
Juice and grated rind of 1/2
  lemon
2 Tbsp. sugar
Salt and pepper to taste

DIRECTIONS
…Quarter and slice carrots into 2 inch strips.
…Cook carrots in boiling water for 8 to 10 minutes until tender.
…Drain.
…Combine butter, lemon juice, and rind.
…Sauté carrots with lemon butter.
…Sprinkle with sugar, salt, and pepper.
…Cook over high heat until glazed.
Serves 6.

SAFE AND SECURE ~ The most important point I always tried to make to my children was that they were safe and secure. When they were young, this meant they could crawl into bed with me whenever they were feeling scared. I believe this laid a foundation of trust so when they were older, they felt comfortable coming to talk to me about anything.

BETH TRIMBLE BURNETT

MINNESOTA APPLE-WALNUT RICE

INGREDIENTS

One 6 oz. package long-grain and wild rice
1/3 c. Madeira wine
2 Tbsp. butter
2 tart cooking apples, peeled and chopped
2 Tbsp. brown sugar
1 c. celery, sliced
1/2 c. walnuts, chopped

DIRECTIONS

…Cook rice according to package directions, using Madeira as part of the liquid.
…Melt butter in a saucepan.
…Add apples and brown sugar.
…Cook apples until they are tender but still hold their shape.
…Stir frequently.
…Stir apple mixture, celery, and walnuts into hot cooked rice.
…Heat one final time.
Serves 6 to 8.

MINNETONKA WILD RICE CASSEROLE

INGREDIENTS

1 c. sour cream
One 8 oz. package long grain wild rice with seasonings
1 large green pepper, diced
1 large onion, diced
1 c. butter
One 8 oz. can mushrooms, drained

DIRECTIONS

…Cook rice according to package directions.
…Sauté pepper and onion.
…Mix rice, onion, pepper, and mushrooms with sour cream.
…Bake at 350 degrees for 30 to 45 minutes.
(May be made a day ahead and baked at dinnertime. French fried onion rings may be used for topping.)
Serves 6 to 8.

NUTTED WILD RICE

INGREDIENTS

1 c. uncooked wild rice
5 1/2 c. defatted chicken
   stock or water
1 c. pecan halves
1 c. yellow raisins
Grated rind of 1 large
   orange
4 scallions, thinly sliced
1/3 c. fresh orange juice
1/2 tsp. salt
Fresh ground pepper

DIRECTIONS

...Put rice in a strainer and
run under cold water to rinse
thoroughly.
...Place rice in a medium-sized
heavy saucepan.
...Add stock and bring to a
rapid boil.
...Reduce heat to a simmer and
cook uncovered for 45 minutes.
...Check at 30 minutes.
...Rice should not be too soft.
...Gently drain.
...Add remaining ingredients
and toss gently.
...Adjust seasonings to taste.
...Let mixture stand for 2 hours
to allow flavors to develop.
...Serve at room temperature.
Serves 6 to 8.

ONIONS SUPREME

INGREDIENTS

7 to 8 c. coarsely chopped onions
1/4 c. butter
1/2 c. uncooked rice
5 c. boiling salted water
1 c. grated Swiss cheese
2/3 c. half-and-half
1 tsp. salt

DIRECTIONS

...Sauté onions in butter until
transparent.
...Cook the rice in boiling water for
5 minutes.
...Drain and mix with the onion.
...Add the cheese and half-and-
half.
...Pour into 3 qt. casserole.
...Bake uncovered for one hour at
325 degrees.
Serves 8.

CREATE A TRADITION ~

Parenting isn't an exact science, it is a series of moments which make memories that last a lifetime. The best way to help create these memories is by creating a tradition. Kids love traditions. They help create order in the chaotic world they are just beginning to discover. Traditions can center around holidays, birthdays, a particular activity, or a meal on a specific day of the week. Bedtime is also a perfect time to create a tradition of reading together or sharing the day's activities. By creating a routine and enjoying the tradition, you have made a memory. Whatever tradition you choose, your children will be the beneficiaries, and so will you.

NANCY ALEXANDER

ORZO PILAF

INGREDIENTS
1 c. orzo (rice shaped pasta)
Vegetable cooking spray
1 Tbsp. olive oil
1 small purple onion, minced
1 red bell pepper, chopped
1 yellow bell pepper, chopped
2 Tbsp. fresh parsley
1/4 tsp. pepper
1/4 tsp. salt
2 cloves garlic, minced
1 1/2 tsp. oregano
1 Tbsp. lemon juice

DIRECTIONS
…Cook orzo and drain.
…Spray a skillet with cooking spray.
…Add olive oil.
…Sauté onion and garlic.
…Mix orzo, onion, garlic, and all remaining ingredients.
…Stir well.
…Bake covered in a 1 1/2 qt. casserole at 350 degrees for 30 minutes.
…Serve hot or cold.
Serves 6 to 8.

PASTA IN WINE SAUCE

INGREDIENTS
4 to 5 oz. pasta
One 10 3/4 oz. can cream of celery
soup
1/2 c. inexpensive white wine
1/2 c. mayonnaise
1/4 c. chopped parsley

DIRECTIONS
...Combine soup, white wine, and
mayonnaise, and pour over cooked
and drained pasta.
...Stir in parsley.
(Baby shrimp or one pound of
browned sausage may be added
to create a main dish.)
Serves 6 to 8.

PECAN PILAF

INGREDIENTS
6 Tbsp. butter
1 c. chopped pecans
1/2 c. chopped onion
2 c. uncooked rice
2 c. chicken stock
2 c. water
1/2 tsp. thyme
3 Tbsp. fresh parsley,
  chopped
Pepper to taste

DIRECTIONS
...Melt 3 Tbsp. butter in a skillet over
medium heat.
...Sauté pecans until lightly browned, 2
to 3 minutes.
...Transfer pecans to a bowl.
...Melt remaining butter in the same
skillet.
...Sauté onions until tender.
...Stir in rice and coat with butter.
...In a saucepan, bring stock, water,
parsley, thyme, pepper, and parsley to a
boil.
...Add mixture to rice.
...Cover and simmer until liquid is
absorbed, approximately 20 minutes.
...Add pecans and fluff with a fork.
...Garnish with extra parsley.
Serves 6 to 8.

PENNE PASTA WITH CHEESE

INGREDIENTS

6 Tbsp. olive oil
1 1/2 c. onion, chopped
1 tsp. garlic, minced
Three 28 oz. cans plum tomatoes,
  drained
2 tsp. basil
1 1/2 tsp. crushed red pepper
2 c. canned low salt chicken broth
1 lb. penne pasta
2 1/2 c. packed grated Havarti cheese
1/3 c. sliced Kalamata olives
1/3 c. fresh basil, finely chopped
1 c. Parmesan cheese

DIRECTIONS

…Preheat oven to 375 degrees.
…Heat 3 Tbsp. olive oil in a heavy Dutch oven over medium heat.
…Add onion and garlic.
…Sauté until onion is translucent.
…Mix in tomatoes, dried basil, and crushed red pepper.
…Bring to a boil.
…Reduce heat to medium.
…Simmer until mixture thickens to a chunky sauce and is reduced to 6 c., stir occasionally for 1 hour and 10 minutes.
…Season with salt and pepper.
(Can be made 2 days ahead.)
…Cover and chill.
…Rewarm over low heat before continuing.
…Preheat oven to 375 degrees.
…Cook pasta in a large pot of boiling salted water until al dente.
…Drain.
…Toss pasta with 3 Tbsp. olive oil.
…Pour sauce on top.
…Toss to blend.
…Mix in Havarti cheese.
…Transfer to 9x13 casserole.
…Sprinkle with olives, then Parmesan cheese.
…Bake 30 minutes.
…Sprinkle with fresh basil.
Serves 8.

ROASTED ASPARAGUS WITH BALSAMIC BROWN BUTTER

INGREDIENTS

40 asparagus spears,
  trimmed (2 lbs.)
Cooking spray
1/4 tsp. Kosher salt
1/8 tsp. black pepper
2 Tbsp. butter (not
  margarine)
2 Tbsp. soy sauce
1 tsp. balsamic vinegar

DIRECTIONS

…Preheat oven to 400 degrees.
…Spray baking pan with cooking
spray.
…Arrange asparagus in a single
layer in pan.
…Sprinkle with salt and pepper.
…Bake at 400 degrees for 12
minutes or until tender.
…Melt butter in a small skillet
over medium heat for 3 minutes or
until lightly browned, shaking pan
occasionally.
…Remove from heat.
…Stir in soy sauce and vinegar.
…Drizzle over asparagus, tossing
well to coat.
…Serve immediately.
Serves 8.

SEASONED NEW POTATOES

INGREDIENTS

1 lb. new potatoes
2 Tbsp. butter
2 Tbsp. fresh dill (or 1/4 c. chopped
fresh parsley)
Salt and pepper to taste

DIRECTIONS

…Wash the potatoes.
…Drop into boiling water and cook
until tender, about 15 minutes.
…Drain well.
…Melt the butter and add potatoes,
stir until coated.
…Add either dill or parsley along
with salt and pepper.
…Toss and serve.
Serves 4.

SPRINGTIME ZUCCHINI WITH PECANS

INGREDIENTS
3 c. zucchini
2 tsp. olive oil
2 garlic cloves, minced
1/4 tsp. pepper
Salt to taste
1/4 c. chopped pecans

DIRECTIONS
…Julienne the zucchini.
…Cook the zucchini and olive oil over medium high heat with the garlic until tender.
…Add pecans and seasonings.
…Toss and serve.
Serves 6.

SWEET POTATO FLUFF

INGREDIENTS
3 medium sweet potatoes (or 2 cans)
1 small banana, well mashed
1/6 c. hot cream
1 Tbsp. butter
1/4 tsp. salt
Marshmallows

DIRECTIONS
…Cook sweet potatoes.
…Peel while hot and mash well.
…Add banana, cream, butter, and salt.
…Pour into baking dish.
…Bake at 350 degrees for 30 minutes.
…Cover with marshmallows and heat again until brown on top.
Serves 6.

THRASHERS 30-DAY MASHED POTATOES

INGREDIENTS
5 lb. red potatoes
8 oz. sour cream
6 oz. cream cheese, softened
1/2 c. butter (1 stick)
Garlic salt
No salt
No pepper

DIRECTIONS
…Boil potatoes with the skins on.
…Mash and stir in sour cream, softened cream cheese, and butter.
…Season with garlic salt.
(Do not use salt or pepper.)
…Place in a glass pan and seal top with plastic wrap.
(Do not use aluminum foil.)
…These potatoes will last for 30 days if kept well covered.
…Doubles easily.
(These are wonderful around the holidays because they can be made ahead and frozen.)
Serves 8 to 10.

TOMATOES IN WINTER

INGREDIENTS

5 medium tomatoes (2 to 3 slices
  per person)
Salt
1/2 c. low fat sour cream
1/4 c. mayonnaise
1/8 tsp. curry
1/4 tsp. dill
2 Tbsp. minced onion

DIRECTIONS

…Wash, core, and thickly slice
tomatoes (3 slices per tomato).
…Drain on paper towel.
…Arrange in a single layer in a
shallow baking pan.
…Salt.
…Combine sour cream,
mayonnaise, curry, dill, and onion.
…Put a spoonful on each tomato
slice.
…Bake at 350 degrees for 20 to 30
minutes until puffed and lightly
brown.
Serves 8.

TRAIL DRIVE CHEESE GRITS

INGREDIENTS

3/4 c. grits, uncooked
3 3/4 c. water
3/4 stick butter
1/2 lb. garlic cheese (or processed
  cheese and 1/4 tsp. garlic powder)
2 drops Tabasco
3/4 tsp. salt
1 Tbsp. Worcestershire sauce

DIRECTIONS

…Cook grits over medium heat
until dry.
…Add butter, cheese, and
seasonings.
…Bake in a buttered casserole
for 45 minutes at 250 degrees.
(Great accompaniment for
barbecue brisket or ham.)
Serves 4 to 6.

ZIPPED-UP ZUCCHINI

INGREDIENTS

4 to 5 medium zucchini, unpeeled
  and sliced 1/4 inch thick
3 medium carrots, shredded
1 medium onion, chopped
1 can cream of chicken soup
1 c. sour cream
1 c. seasoned croutons
Butter

DIRECTIONS

…Boil zucchini until tender
and drain.
…Sauté carrots and onion in
butter until limp.
…Mix soup and sour cream.
…Add to carrots.
…Add 3/4 c. of the croutons and
the zucchini and stir.
…Pour into casserole.
…Put remaining croutons in 1 Tbsp.
of butter and heat until coated.
…Sprinkle on casserole.
…Bake at 350 degrees for 20
to 25 minutes.
Serves 8 to 10.

cake
ice cream
pie &
other

Desserts

PARENT TEACHER CONFERENCES ~
We developed a pre-parent/teacher conference ritual. Before we went we asked our children to list all their classes with all their teachers' names and room numbers. Then we asked them to write down their predictions for what their teachers would say about them: what they will say your strengths are, and what you should work on. We took these worksheets to the conference and made our own notes in different colored ink. When we came home, we compared our notes with our children's pre-conference predictions. It was an enlightening activity for all involved. MARY POWELL YORKE

SING A SONG ~ Ever since our children, Nick, Luke, and Molly were babies, I would sing a special song to each one of them individually before I kissed and hugged them goodnight. As each one outgrew the song, I would use that special time we had established to read a story. The time varied: from five to thirty minutes. But what was special was that it was our alone time together. As they graduated from stories, that time evolved into a period just to talk. We would talk about their day, or whatever was worrying them, or nothing important at all. What was important was the private time outside of our hectic schedule when I could touch base with each of my children. It was always the special moment in my day. MARE CZYZEWSKI-ROCKEFELLER, PH.D.

CAKE

BLACK RUSSIAN CAKE 1

INGREDIENTS
1 package chocolate cake mix
One 4 oz. package instant
  chocolate pudding
1 c. oil
4 eggs
1/4 c. vodka
1/4 c. coffee liqueur

DIRECTIONS
…Mix cake mix, pudding, eggs,
liqueur, and vodka.
…Spoon into greased bundt pan.
…Bake at 325 degrees for 45 to
55 minutes.
…(To make a simple icing, mix
1 c. of powdered sugar with 1 to 3
Tbsp. coffee liqueur and thin with
additional water if necessary.)
…Spread icing on cooled cake or
dust with powdered sugar.

BLACK RUSSIAN CAKE 2

INGREDIENTS
1 package yellow cake mix
One 4 oz. package instant chocolate
  pudding
1 c. oil
4 eggs
1/4 c. vodka
1/4 c. coffee liqueur
2 tsp. vanilla

GLAZE
powdered sugar
coffee liqueur

DIRECTIONS
…Beat cake mix, pudding, oil,
eggs, vodka, liqueur, and vanilla
for two minutes.
…Bake in greased bundt pan at 350
degrees for 50 to 60 minutes.
…Cool in pan.
…For glaze mix 1/2 c. powdered
sugar with enough coffee liqueur to
make glaze.
(Cake freezes well.)

BLUE RIBBON
CHOCOLATE CAKE

INGREDIENTS
1 package devil's food cake mix
One 4 oz. package instant
  chocolate pudding
6 oz. chocolate chips
1 c. water
1/2 c. oil
4 eggs

DIRECTIONS
…Heat oven to 350 degrees.
…Combine all ingredients and
beat for 2 minutes.
…Spread batter into 9x13 pan
or bundt pan.
…Bake 45 minutes.

BULLIED ~ For young boys who are bullied, playtime becomes Hobbesian: nasty and brutish. My son is only 8-years-old, and already we have had a problem with bullies. One actually locked my son in a closet at his home when they were supposed to be playing. He came home from school crying, "He makes us all do bad things. I was mean today. It feels worse to be a bad person than to be picked on. He makes good people do bad things. He's just like Osama bin Ladin!" We talked about it and I told him, "Walk away and don't participate. A good friend will eventually walk away with you." Now I keep him very busy after school so he is not available when this child wants him to come over and play. I have requested that my child be put in another class away from this bully. I volunteer for playground duty. I try to be as vigilant as possible. My son can't solve this problem at his age alone. JANA BARRY

CARROT CAKE

INGREDIENTS

2 c. sugar
1 1/2 c. oil
4 eggs, beaten
2 c. flour
2 tsp. baking soda
2 tsp. baking powder
2 tsp. cinnamon
1 tsp. salt
1 c. pecans, chopped
3 c. grated carrots

DIRECTIONS

…Mix sugar and salad oil.
…Add eggs.
…Add flour, baking soda, baking powder, cinnamon, salt, and mix well.
…Add pecans and carrots.
…Bake in tube pan or flat 9x13 pan at 325 degrees for 30 minutes.

Icing:
…Mix 1 lb. powdered sugar and 8 oz. cream cheese.
…Add 1/4 c. melted butter and 1 tsp. vanilla.
…Beat together and frost immediately.

CHEESECAKE

INGREDIENTS

30 graham cracker squares
1 1/3 c. sugar
2 tsp. sugar
1/3 c. butter
Three 8 oz. packages
  cream cheese
4 eggs, separated
3 tsp. vanilla
8 oz. sour cream

DIRECTIONS

...Allow cream cheese to stand out at room temperature until soft.
...Finely crush graham crackers.
...Blend with 1/3 c. sugar and softened butter.
...Press firmly against bottom and sides of a cheesecake pan.
...Bake at 375 degrees for 8 minutes.
...Cool.
...Place softened cream cheese and 1 c. sugar in a large electric mixer.
...Cream until frothy like whipped cream.
...Add egg yolks and beat well.
...Beat egg whites in a separate bowl.
...Add at a slow speed to ingredients in mixing bowl.
...Pour into crust.
...Bake at 250 degrees for 40 to 45 minutes or until it cracks on top and is barely brown.
...Remove from oven.
...Mix sour cream with 2 Tbsp. sugar and 1 tsp. vanilla.
...Immediately spread on cheesecake when removed from oven.
...Return to oven for 7 minutes.
...Remove from oven, cool, chill, serve.
Serves 12.

CHOCOLATE CHIP POUND CAKE

INGREDIENTS

1 yellow or chocolate cake mix
1 c. sour cream
One 4 oz. package instant chocolate
  pudding mix
1 c. oil
1/2 c. water
1 Tbsp. vanilla
4 eggs
6 oz. chocolate chips

DIRECTIONS

...Mix cake mix, sour cream, pudding mix, oil, water, vanilla, and eggs.
...Add chocolate chips.
...Bake in a bundt pan or angel food cake pan, which has been greased, but not floured.
...Bake at 325 degrees for 45 to 55 minutes.
...Cool on wire rack.
...May be served plain, dusted with powdered sugar, or frosted.

CHOCOLATE SHEET CAKE

FAMILY BUSINESS IS FUN ~ Our children are grown now. Our daughter entered dental school this fall. Our son works in our family's construction business as do I. He learned the importance of work by watching his father build this company from the ground up. We never ask an employee to do anything he or his father would not do themselves. People have asked us how we are able to see each other every day at work and still have so much fun at it. I am very careful when offering opinions or giving advice so I do not hurt the feelings of either young adult. We also rely a great deal on our religion, our church family, and a sense of humor to see the best in each day. Both kids live close enough that we get to see them often and they are happy with their lives and careers. And that is God's blessing for us. BRENDA CLARK

INGREDIENTS
2 c. sugar
2 c. flour
2 c. margarine
4 Tbsp. cocoa
1 c. hot water
1/2 c. buttermilk
1 tsp. soda
1/2 tsp. salt
1 tsp. vanilla
2 eggs
1 tsp. cinnamon

DIRECTIONS
…Sift flour and sugar.
…Bring margarine, cocoa, and water to rolling boil.
…Pour over flour mixture.
…Add buttermilk, soda, salt, vanilla, cinnamon, and eggs.
…Bake in a sheet pan at 375 degrees for 20 minutes.

EASY PARTY CAKE

INGREDIENTS

*1 package Jiffy yellow
    cake mix*
*One 8 oz. package
    cream cheese*
2 c. milk
*One 3 oz. package
    instant vanilla
    pudding mix*
*One 15 oz. can crushed
    pineapple, drained*
*One 8 oz. carton
    Cool Whip*
Coconut flakes

DIRECTIONS (*for cake*)

*…Mix cake according to
directions on package*
…Bake in 9x13 pan or glass dish.
…Cool.

DIRECTIONS (*for topping*)

*…Mix cream cheese and milk
until smooth.*
…Add the pudding mix.
…Beat 3 to 4 minutes.
…Pour over cooled cake.
*…Refrigerate until cooled
and set.*
…Mix cool whip and pineapple.
…Spread over cake.
…Sprinkle with coconut.
…Refrigerate.
(Can be made the day ahead.)

SUCCESS REQUIRES ATTENDANCE ~ To me, motherhood was my job and my vocation. Like any other professional, I believed it was something I had to study and research. One of the most interesting studies I ever read involved why certain high school students excelled. It turned out the common factor was not gender, geographical location, ethnicity, parental income, or occupation. It was the <u>number of times</u> the parent crossed the threshold of the school for an event, not just their own child's events, but any school activity. By doing this, the parents knew the teachers, the other students, and what was happening at the school. So, I made school my second home, attending events as often as possible. LINDA POLLY

GERMAN CHOCOLATE POUND CAKE

INGREDIENTS

One 4 oz. package
   German sweet
   chocolate
2 c. sugar
1 c. shortening
4 eggs
2 tsp. vanilla
1 c. buttermilk
3 c. flour
1/2 tsp. soda
1 tsp. salt

DIRECTIONS

...Partially melt chocolate in a double boiler.
...Remove from hot water and stir until chocolate is melted.
...In separate bowl, cream sugar and shortening.
...Add eggs, vanilla, and buttermilk.
...Sift flour, soda, and salt.
...Add to shortening and sugar and mix well.
...Stir in chocolate.
...Pour batter into greased and floured bundt pan.
...Bake at 300 degrees for about 1 1/2 hours.
...Remove from pan.
...While still hot, place under tightly fitting cover until thoroughly cooled.

GRANNY'S GREEN APPLE CAKE

INGREDIENTS

3 c. flour
2 c. sugar
1 tsp. salt
1 tsp. baking soda
1/2 tsp. cinnamon
1 c. oil
1/2 c. milk
3 eggs
1 tsp. vanilla
3 green apples, peeled
   and diced
1 c. chopped walnuts
1/2 c. raisins

Lemon Glaze:
1 c. powdered sugar
2 Tbsp. lemon juice

DIRECTIONS

...In a large mixing bowl, blend first 9 ingredients.
...Beat on low for 3 minutes.
...Fold in apples, nuts, and raisins.
...Pour batter into 10 inch tube pan.
...Bake at 350 degrees for 1 hour and 15 minutes.
...Cool cake in pan for 10 minutes.
...Remove from pan and cool completely.
...Mix powdered sugar and lemon juice and spoon over cake.

HOLIDAY BRUNCH CAKE

INGREDIENTS
1 c. butter
5 eggs, unbeaten
1 c. buttermilk
1 tsp. vanilla
2 c. pecan pieces
3 c. flour
1 tsp. soda
1 tsp. cinnamon
1 tsp. allspice
1 tsp. nutmeg
1/2 tsp. salt

Glaze:
1 c. sugar
1/3 c. water

DIRECTIONS (*for cake*)
…*Cream sugar, butter, and eggs.*
…*Add dry ingredients, vanilla, and buttermilk alternately, beating only until smooth.*
…*Add nuts and bake in a bundt or tube pan that has been greased and lightly floured on bottom only.*
…*Bake at 325 degrees for 1 1/2 hours.*
…*Pour on glaze.*
…*Invert and cool.*

DIRECTIONS (*for glaze*)
Combine sugar and water. Bring to a boil and pour over hot cake.

JEWISH COFFEECAKE

INGREDIENTS
1 box white or sour cream cake mix
One 3 oz. pkg. instant vanilla pudding mix
1/2 c. oil
4 eggs
1 c. sour cream
2 tsp. vanilla

Topping
3/4 c. chopped nuts
1/2 c. sugar
2 tsp. cinnamon

DIRECTIONS
…*Combine cake mix, pudding, oil, eggs, sour cream, and vanilla.*
…*Blend together nuts, sugar, and cinnamon for topping.*
…*Alternate layers of cake filling and sugar topping.*
…*Bake at 350 degrees for 50 to 55 minutes.*

KANSAS DIRT CAKE

INGREDIENTS
One 16 oz. pkg. Oreo cookies, crushed
1/2 c. margarine
One 8 oz. package cream cheese
1/2 c. powdered sugar
Two 3 oz. packages instant
  vanilla pudding
3 c. milk
One 8 oz. carton frozen dessert
  topping, thawed
1 tsp. vanilla

DIRECTIONS
…Place half of crushed cookies in
the bottom of a 9x13 casserole dish.
…Melt margarine and cream cheese.
…Add powdered sugar and vanilla.
…In a bowl, combine pudding
mixes and milk, then add to cheese
mixture.
…Pour over cookies.
…"Frost" with dessert topping.
…Top with remaining crushed
cookies and chill.
…No baking required.

LEMON POPPY SEED CAKE

INGREDIENTS
One 1 lb. 3 oz. package
  lemon cake mix
One 4 1/2 oz. package instant
  lemon pudding mix
4 eggs
3/4 c. oil
3/4 c. lemonade
2 Tbsp. poppy seeds
Powdered sugar

DIRECTIONS
…Combine all ingredients.
…Beat with electric mixer
for 3 minutes.
…Pour batter into 2 loaf
pans.
…Bake at 350 degrees for
35 to 40 minutes.
…Make a glaze with
powdered sugar and
lemonade and pour
over hot cake.

MOM'S INSTANT STRAWBERRY SHORTCAKE

INGREDIENTS
10 buttermilk refrigerator biscuits
2 1/2 Tbsp. butter
2 1/2 tsp. sugar
1 qt. fresh strawberries, sweetened
  with sugar (Or 10 oz. box sliced
  strawberries with sugar)
Whipped cream

DIRECTIONS
…Flatten all biscuits to approximately
3 1/2 to 4 inches.
…Place 5 biscuits on greased cookie sheet.
…Top each with remaining 5 biscuits.
…Cook as directed on package or until
golden brown.
…Place biscuits on serving plates.
…Place a pat of butter in the center and
on top of each biscuit.
…Sprinkle 1/2 tsp. of sugar on each pat of
butter.
…Spoon strawberries between and on top
of the biscuit.
…Top with whipped cream.

CHANGE OF SCENERY ~ Every mother of a teenage girl knows there is a moment when an evil wizard curses their little princess and turns her into a smug, sarcastic, know-it-all. It is as if all the love and affection you have poured into your child has spoiled her. What is needed is a change of perspective. Our daughter was an only child, who was adored (worshipped) by all members of her extended family. She grew up in this bubble. When she was sixteen, the curse hit. That summer we sent her to Paraguay with a foreign exchange program (AFS). It cured her. I was ready to smack the girl I sent. I loved the young woman who returned to us. To this day she says it was the best thing she did in high school, maybe in her entire life. HELEN CROW

CAR POOLS ~ For over eighteen years I was a soccer, tennis, golf, baseball, football, basketball, cello, handbells, drums, and piano mom. I spent more time in the car than Suzanne Somers in *American Graffiti*. The best "mom" lesson learned while driving was to turn the radio off and listen. Sometimes the little voice from the back seat will ask you questions or talk about problems they would never discuss face-to-face. Another lesson about car pools: when my children became teenagers, I learned to refrain from making comments of any kind because if I did speak up I became "visible" and the conversation stopped. You can find out so much more about your children by staying quiet in the car. Private talks can always take place later. WIDGE YAGER

ORANGE COFFEECAKE

INGREDIENTS

1 yellow cake mix
1 package instant vanilla pudding
3/4 c. orange juice
3/4 c. oil
4 eggs
1 tsp. vanilla

DIRECTIONS

...Beat all ingredients together for 2 minutes.
...Pour 1/3 batter into well greased tube pan.
...Sprinkle 1/2 filler (made of 1/2 c. sugar, 2 tsp. cinnamon, and 1/2 c. chopped pecans) over batter.
...Continue filling pan, alternating ingredients until used.
...Bake at 350 degrees for one hour.
...Cake can be glazed with a mixture of vanilla, butter, and powdered sugar.

PIONEER PUMPKIN CAKE

INGREDIENTS

2 c. sugar
2 c. flour
2 tsp. cinnamon
1 tsp. soda
2 tsp. baking powder
1/2 tsp. salt
4 eggs
1 c. oil
One 16 oz. can pumpkin
3 oz. cream cheese
3/4 c. butter
1 tsp. vanilla
1 tsp. milk
1 lb. powdered sugar
Chopped nuts

DIRECTIONS

...Combine the first 8 ingredients.
...Add pumpkin and mix well.
...Pour into greased and floured bundt pan.
...Bake at 325 degrees for 30 minutes.
...For frosting combine cream cheese, butter, vanilla, and milk.
...Gradually add powdered sugar to reach desired spreading consistency.
...Spread on cooled cake.
...Sprinkle with chopped nuts.

FREE TIME ~ I would advise young mothers to limit the number of activities their children participate in. Sometimes they are "overly-programmed": every minute of every day is planned out. This often results in children who do not know how to entertain themselves. Children need time to play and just be children. PAULA BAUM

SPEAK SOFTLY AND CARRY A BIG CLUB ~ Our two daughters have always been good about adhering to their curfews. On the other hand, our son failed miserably at this. After repeated infractions and having been warned by his father that if he broke curfew again, the "club" would be put on his car, the warning came to pass. Without saying a word, his dad placed the club on our son's steering wheel and when Randy woke up the next day to go to his girlfriend's house, he was shocked at what he saw. The club stayed on for the entire weekend, and he suddenly thought twice about ever being late for curfew in the future. PAULA BAUM

PUMPKIN CAKE

POPPY SEED BUNDT CAKE

INGREDIENTS

1/4 c. poppy seeds
1 c. water
1/2 c. oil
1 package yellow cake mix
3 eggs
Powdered sugar
Lemon juice

DIRECTIONS

…Soak poppy seeds in water for one hour.
…Blend cake mix, oil, eggs, and poppy seeds.
…Pour into greased, floured bundt pan or 9x13 flat pan.
…Bake at 350 degrees for 40 to 45 minutes or until toothpick comes out clean.
…Cool 20 minutes in pan.
…Remove from pan and spread glaze made of powdered sugar and lemon juice.

PUMPKIN CAKE

INGREDIENTS

6 large eggs
1 large can pumpkin (3 cups)
1 1/2 c. sugar
3/4 tsp. salt
2 tsp. cinnamon
1 tsp. ginger
1/2 tsp. ground cloves
1 can evaporated milk

Topping:
1 yellow cake mix
1 stick margarine (not melted)

DIRECTIONS

…Beat eggs lightly.
…Add pumpkin.
…Add sugar, salt, cinnamon, ginger, cloves, and evaporated milk.
…Pour into greased 9x13 pan.
…For the topping, combine cake mix and unmelted margarine, cut into small pieces.
…Sprinkle over pumpkin mix.
…Bake at 350 degrees for 50 to 60 minutes.

SHERRY POUND CAKE

INGREDIENTS

One 1 lb. 3 oz. package yellow cake mix.
One 4 1/2 oz. package instant vanilla pudding mix
4 eggs
3/4 c. oil
3/4 c. cooking sherry
1 tsp. nutmeg

DIRECTIONS

…Combine all ingredients.
…Beat with electric mixer for 3 minutes.
…Pour batter into greased and floured bundt cake pan.
…Bake at 350 degrees for 45 to 50 minutes.
…Sprinkle with powdered sugar.
…Serve with fresh berries.

SOUR CREAM COFFEECAKE

INGREDIENTS
1 1/2 c. butter
1 7/8 c. sugar
3 eggs, beaten
1 1/2 c. sour cream
1 1/2 tsp. vanilla
3 c. sifted flour
1 1/2 tsp. baking powder
3/4 tsp. baking soda

Topping:
1 1/8 c. chopped pecans
7 1/2 tsp. sugar
1 1/2 tsp. cinnamon

DIRECTIONS
…Cream butter and sugar.
…Add beaten eggs, sour cream, and vanilla.
…Beat well.
…Gradually add dry mixture and beat thoroughly.
…Mix topping ingredients together.
…Butter and flour 9x13 pan.
…Spread half of batter into pan.
…Sprinkle half of topping over batter.
…Cover with remaining batter.
…Sprinkle remaining topping.
…Bake at 350 degrees for 35 minutes or until knife comes out clean.
…Sprinkle with powdered sugar.
…Cool.
…Cut into squares.

STEPHENSON'S APPLE FARM CAKE

INGREDIENTS
1/4 c. shortening
1 c. sugar
1 egg
4 c. apples, chopped
1/3 c. raisins
1 c. flour
1 tsp. baking soda
1/4 tsp. salt
1 tsp. cinnamon
1/2 tsp. nutmeg
1/4 tsp. cloves

DIRECTIONS
…Cream shortening and sugar.
…Add egg, apples, and raisins.
…Sift all other ingredients and add to apple mixture.
…Mix well.
(Batter will be very thick.)
…Spread into greased 9x13 pan.
…Bake at 325 degrees for 45 minutes.
…Can be topped with ice cream or cream cheese frosting.

STRAWBERRY CAKE

INGREDIENTS
1 package white cake mix
1 package strawberry gelatin (3 oz.)
4 eggs beaten
2/3 c. oil
One 18 oz. package frozen
  strawberries with juice.
1/2 c. water
Powdered sugar

DIRECTIONS
...Mix all ingredients.
...Pour into greased and floured
bundt cake pan.
...Bake at 350 degrees for 45 to 50
minutes.
...Use additional strawberry juice
and powdered sugar to make a
glaze for the cake.

SUNSHINE ORANGE CAKE...

INGREDIENTS
1 box yellow or butter cake mix
3 eggs
3/4 c. oil
One 11 oz. can mandarin oranges,
  including juice

DIRECTIONS
...Mix cake mix, eggs, oil, and oranges for
2 minutes.
...Pour mixture into either a 9x13 or two 8
inch pans that are greased and floured.
...Bake at 325 degrees for 30 to 35 minutes.

...AND FROSTING

INGREDIENTS
One 20 oz. can crushed pineapple, drained
One 3 oz. package instant vanilla pudding
Two 8 oz. cartons frozen dessert topping,
  thawed

DIRECTIONS
...Mix dessert topping, pineapple, and
pudding mix.
...Frost cooled cake.
...Refrigerate.

TWO-HUNDRED-DOLLAR CARROT CAKE...

INGREDIENTS
1 c. oil
1 c. sugar
3 eggs
1 1/3 c. flour
1 1/2 tsp. baking powder
1 1/2 tsp. baking soda
1 1/2 tsp. cinnamon
2 c. grated carrots
1 c. walnuts, chopped

DIRECTIONS
...Preheat oven to 350 degrees.
...Grease and flour a 10" bundt pan.
...Mix oil and sugar with electric mixer.
...Add eggs slowly.
...Add flour and spices on low speed.
...Stir in carrots and nuts.
...Bake for 1 hour.
...Cool 10 to 15 minutes.
...Remove from pan.

...AND ICING

INGREDIENTS
1/4 c. butter
2 tsp. vanilla
One 8 oz. package cream cheese
2 c. powdered sugar
1/2 c. walnuts, chopped

DIRECTIONS
...Mix everything together except nuts.
...Split cake in 3 layers and frost, leaving the sides of cake unfrosted.
...Sprinkle nuts on top of cake.

FOCUS, FOCUS, FOCUS ~ I don't profess to be an expert on raising children, but I do value the profession of motherhood above almost all others. Having been raised by two loving parents who are also educators, I would have to say the most important gift you can give your children is to focus on them exclusively when you are with them. So many things compete for our attention and time (and for theirs as well) that we are often frazzled and unable to hear what our children are really telling us. Children truly are gifts for us to admire and appreciate each day—but only if we slow down long enough to experience their world alongside them in the simplest of ways. Put down the phone and read a book, go on a walk, or just play in the sand—together. KRISTIN CHANAY

ICE CREAM

BUTTER-NUT ICE CREAM

INGREDIENTS
2 1/4 c. sugar
6 Tbsp. flour
1/2 tsp. salt
5 c. milk, scalded
6 eggs
4 c. heavy cream
5 tsp. vanilla
2 c. almonds, pecans,
  or walnuts sautéed in
   3 Tbsp. butter

DIRECTIONS
…Combine sugar, flour, and salt in a saucepan.
…Slowly stir in hot milk.
…Cook over low heat for about 10 minutes, stirring constantly until mixture is thickened.
…Mix a small amount of hot mixture into beaten eggs.
…Then combine egg and hot mixture and cook 1 minute longer.
…Chill.
…Add cream and vanilla.
…Pour into freezer and churn for 15 minutes or until ice cream is mushy.
…Add chopped nuts and continue freezing according to freezer directions.

CHOCOLATE ICE CREAM

INGREDIENTS
1/3 c. sugar
6 Tbsp. flour
1/2 tsp. salt
3 c. milk, scalded
6 eggs
4 c. heavy cream
3 c. chocolate syrup
5 tsp. vanilla

DIRECTIONS
…Combine sugar, flour, and salt in a saucepan.
…Slowly stir in hot milk.
…Cook over low heat for about 10 minutes, stirring constantly until mixture is thickened.
…Mix a small amount of hot mixture into beaten eggs.
…Then add this to the hot mixture and cook 1 minute longer.
…Chill.
…Add cream, chocolate, and vanilla.
…Freeze in electric freezer as directed.

CRISPY ICE CREAM

INGREDIENTS
1/2 c. butter
1 c. pecans
3/4 c. brown sugar
2 1/2 c. rice chex cereal
1 1/2 qt. vanilla ice cream

DIRECTIONS
…Coarsely chop pecans and brown in butter.
…Add brown sugar.
…Crush the cereal and mix with nuts.
…Put half of mix on the bottom of an 8x10 pan.
…Spread softened ice cream over mixture.
…Top with the rest of the mix and freeze.
…Serve with whipped cream and drizzle with caramel sauce.

VANILLA ICE CREAM

INGREDIENTS
2 1/4 c. sugar
6 Tbsp. flour
1/2 tsp. salt
5 c. milk, scalded
6 eggs
4 c. heavy cream
5 tsp. vanilla

DIRECTIONS
…Combine, sugar, flour, and salt in a saucepan.
…Slowly stir in hot milk.
…Cook over low heat for about 10 minutes, stirring constantly until mixture is thickened.
…Mix a small amount of hot mixture into beaten eggs.
…Then combine egg and hot mixture and cook 1 minute longer.
…Chill.
…Add cream and vanilla.
…Pour into freezer.
(This is a popular farm family recipe.)

YUMMY COFFEE ICE CREAM

INGREDIENTS
4 tsp. instant coffee
2 1/2 c. sugar
1/4 tsp. salt
2 Tbsp. flour
2 1/2 c. milk
2 1/2 c. coffee, brewed
6 egg yolks, slightly beaten
5 c. heavy cream
5 tsp. vanilla
1/4 c. coffee liqueur (optional)

DIRECTIONS
…Combine instant coffee, sugar, salt, and flour in a saucepan.
…Gradually pour in milk and brewed coffee, stirring constantly.
…Cook over low heat until slightly thickened.
…Pour some of the hot mixture over the eggs and blend well.
…Add to hot mixture.
…Continue to cook for one more minute and chill.
…Add cream and vanilla.
…Freeze in ice cream freezer according to directions.

PIE

CHERRY CRANBERRY PIE

INGREDIENTS
One 21 oz. can cherry pie filling
2 c. fresh or frozen cranberries
3/4 c. sugar
2 Tbsp. flour
2 pie crusts

DIRECTIONS
…Heat oven to 425 degrees.
…Combine cranberries, sugar, and flour in a bowl.
…Stir in cherry pie filling.
…Pour into pie shell.
…Cut slits in second crust and top the pie.
…Crimp edges.
…Bake 50 minutes or until golden brown.

CRANBERRY PECAN PIE

INGREDIENTS
3 eggs
1 c. dark corn syrup
2/3 c. sugar
1/4 c. butter
1/8 tsp. salt
1 c. fresh cranberries, chopped
1 c. pecans
1 unbaked pie shell

DIRECTIONS
…Preheat oven to 325 degrees.
…Beat eggs in a bowl until blended.
…Add syrup, sugar, butter, and salt.
…Sprinkle cranberries and pecans in pastry shell.
…Pour syrup mixture over filling.
…Bake 50 to 55 minutes or until a knife comes out clean.

DERBY PIE

INGREDIENTS
1 c. granulated sugar
1/2 c. flour
1 stick butter, softened
1/2 tsp. vanilla
2 Tbsp. bourbon
2 eggs, slightly beaten
2/3 c. chocolate chips
2/3 c. chopped pecans
1 unbaked deep dish pie shell
Whipped cream

DIRECTIONS
…Mix flour and sugar.
…Add eggs, butter, vanilla, bourbon, chocolate chips, and pecans.
…Pour into unbaked pie shell.
…Bake at 325 degrees for 50 minutes.
…Garnish with whipped cream and a sprig of mint.

FRENCH SILK PIE

INGREDIENTS
1/2 c. butter
3/4 c. sugar
1 oz. bitter chocolate
1 tsp. vanilla
2 eggs
9 inch baked pie shell

DIRECTIONS
...Thoroughly cream room-
temperature butter with sugar.
...Blend in melted chocolate and
vanilla.
...Add eggs, one at a time.
...Beat on high with electric mixer
for 5 minutes after each addition.
...Pour into baked, cooled pie shell.
...Chill 2 hours before serving.
...Top with whipped cream.

FROZEN MARGARITA PIE

INGREDIENTS
1 graham cracker pie crust
1 can sweetened condensed milk
1 c. sliced strawberries
1/3 c. frozen margarita mix, thawed
2 c. dairy topping

DIRECTIONS
...Mix milk, strawberries, margarita
mix and dairy topping.
...Pour into pie shell.
...Garnish with topping, whole
strawberries, and lime slices.
...Refrigerate.

HOT LEMON PIE

INGREDIENTS
2 lemons
4 eggs
1 1/2 c. sugar
1/2 c. butter
1 tsp. vanilla
1 unbaked pastry shell

DIRECTIONS
...Cut the ends off the 2 lemons.
...Cut into pieces.
...Remove seeds.
...Chop in blender until chunky.
...Add eggs, sugar, butter, and
vanilla.
...Beat until almost smooth.
...Pour into unbaked pie shell.
...Bake for 45 minutes at 350
degrees.

IRISH BLESSING ~ May the road rise to meet you. May the wind be always at your back. May the rain fall soft upon your fields. And until we meet again, may God hold you in the palm of His hand.

LAZY DAY LEMON PIE

INGREDIENTS
1 graham cracker pie crust
1 can sweetened condensed milk
One 6 oz. can frozen lemonade concentrate
One 8 oz. container dairy topping

DIRECTIONS
…Mix milk, lemonade, and dairy topping.
…Pour into pie crust.
…Refrigerate.
…Decorate with lemon slices and fresh mint.

THE ORIGINAL PLAN WAS TO GIVE MY SON AND HIS WIFE A NIGHT OUT ONCE A WEEK ~ Their two small sons and baby-sitting funds limited their "dates" so they jumped at the idea. I, in turn, thought I was a great mother and mother-in-law.

The months of these weekly nights out have turned into years. I now know my grandson's favorite games, books and thoughts. They know my favorite poems and can recite them with me. We have great discussions about their pets, their schools, and how butterflies migrate. Each week it is different. Their faces beam when I walk in the door – they are anxious to tell me their latest news.

I have learned that mac and cheese or peanut butter sandwiches make a great dinner especially when we are laughing at our secret jokes.

My heart is full when I drive home remembering the fun we three had together. We have bonded and it is a time that the boys and I will remember all our lives. Do not let an opportunity such as this slip away. JAN BENSON

NEVER-FAIL PECAN PIE

INGREDIENTS
1 c. light corn syrup
2 Tbsp. butter, melted
1/8 tsp. salt
3 eggs, slightly beaten
1 c. sugar
1 tsp. vanilla
1 c. pecans
One 9 inch unbaked deep dish pie shell

DIRECTIONS
…Preheat oven to 400 degrees.
…Mix all ingredients, adding the pecans last.
…Pour into pie shell.
…Bake for 15 minutes at 400 degrees.
…Lower temperature to 350 degrees and bake 45 additional minutes.
(This pie freezes well. Serve warm with real whipped cream or vanilla ice cream.)

BUSINESS AND FRIENDSHIP DO MIX ~ I bought a home from a good friend twenty-five years ago. We closed the deal "on a handshake" and then told our husbands. No financial records traded hands. She had my word and I had hers. That was all either of us needed. We continued to be neighbors so my children knew this woman and heard this story as they grew up. This year this same friend was displaced from her home and I have rented her a home I own once again "on a handshake" and our word. My now grown children can see from this example that women can be friends and business associates for a lifetime. Integrity is the key. MARY DORSEY WANLESS

OTHER

AMARETTO FUDGE SAUCE

INGREDIENTS
One 14 oz. can sweetened condensed milk
12 oz. package chocolate chips
2/3 c. Amaretto

DIRECTIONS
...Melt chocolate chips and sweetened condensed milk over low heat.
...Remove from heat and stir in Amaretto until smooth.
...Refrigerate.
...If sauce becomes too thick, thin with a small amount of milk.

BAKLAVA

INGREDIENTS
1 lb. filo/phyllo
1 lb. butter (not margarine)
1 lb. ground nuts (almonds or walnuts)
2 c. honey
4 c. sugar
1 to 2 c. water
Ground cinnamon
Ground cloves

DIRECTIONS
...Preheat oven to 400 degrees.
...Mix nuts, 2 c. sugar, 2 tsp. cinnamon, and 2 tsp. cloves.
...Set aside.
...Melt butter in a large pan.
...Mix honey, 2 c. sugar, water, 1 tsp. cinnamon, and 1 tsp. cloves.
...Bring to a boil.
...Reduce heat and simmer 20 minutes.
...Cut filo to fit 9x13 pan.
...Brush bottom of pan with butter.
...Cover with 2 to 3 filo leaves.
...Butter filo.
...Sprinkle half of nut mixture on filo.
...Repeat layers.
...End with buttered filo layer.
...Allow to rest 1 to 2 minutes.
...Cut into 1 1/2 inch squares or diamonds.
...Bake 30 to 40 minutes until golden brown.
...Remove from oven.
...Pour hot syrup over pastry while it's hot.
...Allow to rest at least 30 minutes before cutting and removing from pan to serve. (May be frozen.)

BERRY CRISP

INGREDIENTS
4 c. fruit (i.e. apples,
peaches, blueberries,
cherries, raspberries)
1/2 c. brown sugar
1 tsp. cinnamon
1/3 c. flour
1 c. rolled oats
1/2 tsp. salt
1/3 c. butter, melted

DIRECTIONS
...Place 4 c. of the fruit of your
choice in a 9x9 baking dish.
...Mix all other ingredients
together.
...Sprinkle on top of the fruit.
...Bake at 375 degrees for 30
minutes.

BUSTER BAR DESSERT

INGREDIENTS
42 Oreo cookies
1/2 c. butter, melted
1/2 gal. vanilla ice cream
2 c. powdered sugar
One 13 oz. can evaporated
milk
2/3 c. chocolate chips
1 tsp. vanilla
1 c. Spanish peanuts
One 8 oz. carton frozen
dessert topping

DIRECTIONS
...Crush cookies and mix
with butter.
...Spread evenly in the
bottom of a 9x13 pan.
...Press down and place in
freezer until firm.
...Layer ice cream over crust.
...Freeze again.
...For the next layer, mix
together in a saucepan
powdered sugar, evaporated
milk, chocolate chips, and
margarine.
...Boil for 8 minutes, stirring
constantly.
...Cool and add vanilla.
...Spread over ice cream.
...Sprinkle on peanuts.
...Spread thawed dessert
topping over peanut layer.
...Sprinkle on extra cookie
crumbs (if desired).
...Cover with foil and freeze.

CHOCOLATE MOUSSE

INGREDIENTS
One 12 oz. package chocolate chips
1/2 c. crème de cocoa
6 eggs, separated
1/8 tsp. cream of tartar

DIRECTIONS
…Melt chocolate chips in microwave or double boiler.
…Slowly stir in crème de cocoa until mixture is smooth.
…Remove from heat and slowly stir in beaten egg yolks.
…Cool mixture to room temperature.
…Beat egg whites, adding cream of tartar, until stiff.
…Fold into chocolate mixture.
…Pour into goblets and chill.
Serves 4 to 6.

CHOCOLATE DIPPED STRAWBERRIES

INGREDIENTS
2 pints fresh strawberries
One 12 oz. package chocolate chips
2 Tbsp. oil

DIRECTIONS
…Wash and dry strawberries, leaving stems.
…Melt chocolate in a double boiler.
…Add oil and mix well.
…Leave stems on fruit.
…Dip strawberries in chocolate and place on cookie sheet lined with waxed paper.
…Refrigerate.
(You may substitute white chocolate chips.)

CHOCOLATE GLAZE

INGREDIENTS
2 c. powdered sugar
1 tsp. vanilla
2 oz. unsweetened chocolate, melted
2 Tbsp. butter, softened
3 to 4 Tbsp. milk

DIRECTIONS
…In a medium bowl beat together sugar, vanilla, chocolate, and butter.
…Add enough milk to make glaze consistency.
…For an even glaze, pour into a small plastic freezer bag.
…Snip off one corner to make a small hole.
…Squeeze glaze gently through opening.

FIND A GOOD EXAMPLE ~ When we moved to this city I knew only two couples and had no family close by. I was new at parenting with a four-year-old and a four-month-old. I needed help. So I looked for other mothers I admired and observed how they raised their children. I found exceptional teachers who mentored my kids far beyond their job description and are now my good friends. I found great neighborhoods and families of all ages to teach me parenting skills.

We have moved several times since those early days but if I needed 'a village', now I would only need to come out my front door and look around at all the special friends whose homes I can see from my porch.

If I were raising small children now I would only need to look next door to find a shining example of how best to raise the typical midwestern family. Meet the Franklins: Mike, Katy and kids Adam, Sarah, Mary Kate, Claire, and baby brother Luke Robert who has just arrived. Dad works hard. Mom stays at home. The kids are all good friends with each other, get excellent grades, have a very busy schedule of activities, take their religion seriously, and are the most polite children I have ever known.

*

How did they do it? I've watched this family grow up over the years and I know it is by example. Dad is a physician and works very long hours. The example is that nothing is easy. Mom helps everyone and has the kindest heart. The example is "do unto others..."

Everything they do is with a thought to family. All their activities at home, in their recreation, and on vacation, revolve around the family.

So find a family like the Franklins whom you admire and watch how they do it. And if you are lucky, they will live right next door.

LINDA POLLY

'Jammies,' Pink Lemonade, and Marshmallows ~ We waited for a long time to become grandparents. To our joy six healthy, beautiful grandchildren were born in our family in just a few short years. My days were full just watching our own children be such good parents and helping out whenever I was asked. Our lives were shattered one month ago when our little three-year-old Morgan Pollak spiked a fever, was hospitalized, and suddenly died. This was the child that talked in phrases and short sentences before her first birthday. She had long black ringlets that bounced when she walked. We were stopped many times by strangers who were drawn to her personality. She learned nursery rhymes and songs on her own and recited them to us. During her illness, she would wake up from the fever and talk double-time to make up for not be-ing able to talk while she was sick. We found some peace in the autopsy report that gave the cause of death as Myocarditis, a rare viral condition for which there is no cure. The pathologist said, "It's believed that it is not so much the virus itself, which differs from person to person, as it is the combination of the virus and its host."

I have no answers for why she was taken from our family. I do know she taught us many things in her short life. As I raced to the hospital on that last night, I remembered that I had talked to her that evening planning an overnight, and she had asked, "Will you bring your 'jammies'? And will you bring TREATS!?" Treats for Morgan were pink lemonade, raisons, marshmallows, and fish crackers. I had just made her birthday cake and asked what kind she wanted. She said, "Any cake with sprinkles on it." So, we had cupcakes with sprinkles. She found such joy in the simplest things. I try to do the same.

I have no regrets because I carried story books in my car to read to her every time I saw her. We played games, sang songs, shopped, and ate "treats." I know as a mother I must be strong for my daughter Shelley Clark Pollak and her husband David who must raise their infant son and the rest of our family. I listen everyday hoping to hear something to make our family feel better.

We gained comfort from the friends who flew in from around the country for the funeral, the cards, flowers, the doctors and nurses from the ER who came to the visitation, and the firm belief that she is in a better place and I will someday see her again.

We will gather for the holidays and special family dinners. The food we serve will probably be the same as everyone else we know. But from now on there will be an extra table of "treats" which will always include pink lemonade, raisons, marshmallows, and fish crackers.

And cupcakes with sprinkles! LINDA MARLING

CINNAMON SUGAR ROLL-UPS

INGREDIENTS
1 loaf white sandwich bread (designer bread
    does not work)
One 8 oz. package cream cheese
3/4 c. butter, melted
Sugar
Cinnamon

DIRECTIONS
…Cut the crust off the bread slices.
…Spread the slices with softened cream cheese.
…Roll up (like a cigar).
…Roll in melted butter.
…Roll in cinnamon-sugar mixture.
(May be frozen at this point.)
…Heat oven to 350 degrees.
…Place roll-ups on a cookie sheet.
…Bake 5 minutes.
…Turn over and bake 5 to 7 minutes longer.
…Roll-ups will crisp as they cool.

FROZEN FRUIT SALAD/DESSERT

INGREDIENTS

1 can cherry pie filling
One 12 oz. can crushed pineapple, undrained
1/4 c. chopped fresh apple, unpeeled
One 8 oz. can fruit cocktail, drained
1 can sweetened condensed milk
One 12 oz. carton frozen dairy topping

DIRECTIONS

…Mix all ingredients together and freeze in a 9x13 pan or 2 smaller pans.
(This will keep for several days and may be used as a salad or dessert.)
Serves 16 to 20.

FRUIT PIZZA

INGREDIENTS

1 tube refrigerated sugar cookie dough
One 8 oz. package cream cheese, softened
1/2 c. sugar
1/2 tsp. vanilla
2 Tbsp. tapioca
Various fruits, drain well, reserving juices
(i.e. peaches, blueberries, strawberries, mandarin oranges, pears, and pineapple)

DIRECTIONS

…For the crust, flatten the sugar cookie dough onto a lightly greased pizza pan.
…Bake 10 to 12 minutes at 375 degrees until lightly browned.
…Mix cream cheese, sugar, and vanilla.
…Spread on cooled crust.
…Arrange colorful fruit of your choice around the top of the pizza.
…Heat reserved fruit juices with 2 Tbsp. tapioca until mixture thickens.
…Allow to cool.
…Pour over fruit to seal the top.

GRANNY'S PIE CRUST

INGREDIENTS
2 c. flour
1 tsp. salt
1/3 c. milk
1/2 c. vegetable oil

DIRECTIONS
…In a small deep bowl, mix flour
and salt.
…Make a well in the center of the
flour.
…Add the milk and then the oil.
…Cut with a fork until it just
begins to stick together.
…Divide in half.
…Roll each crust out between two
sheets of waxed paper.

INDIAN PUDDING

INGREDIENTS
1/3 c. cornmeal
5 c. milk, divided
1/3 c. molasses
1/4 c. sugar
1 tsp. salt
1 tsp. ginger

DIRECTIONS
…Cook cornmeal and 4 c. milk in
double boiler for 20 minutes.
…Add all other ingredients
except the 5th cup of milk.
…Bake in a greased baking dish
at 325 degrees for 3 hours.
…At the end of the first two
hours, stir in 5th cup of cold milk.
…Bake one more hour.
…Serve hot with vanilla ice
cream.

IRISH WHISKEY SAUCE

INGREDIENTS
2 Tbsp. butter
2 Tbsp. flour
1 c. cream
1/4 c. sugar
1 Tbsp. whiskey

DIRECTIONS
…Melt butter.
…Stir in flour.
…Add sugar and heat until
dissolved.
…Add cream and whiskey.
…Pour over slices of your
favorite pound cake.
…Dust with powdered sugar
and sprinkle each serving
with fresh berries or fruit.

KANSAS PERSIMMON PUDDING

INGREDIENTS
2 qt. sweet milk
1 qt. ripe persimmons
1 1/2 pt. sugar
1 tsp. soda
3 eggs
1/4 c. butter
1 c. flour

DIRECTIONS
…*Pour milk over thoroughly ripe persimmons (picked after frost).*
…*Mash and rub through a colander.*
…*Add sugar, soda, eggs, butter, and flour.*
…*Mix together well.*
…*Pour into a deep granite pan or crock.*
…*Bake three hours in moderate oven (350 degrees).*
…*When cold, serve with rich cream. (Can be served with vanilla ice cream.)*

LEMON CURD FILLING

INGREDIENTS
1 c. sugar
6 egg yolks, beaten
1/2 c. fresh lemon juice
1 Tbsp. grated lemon rind
1/2 c. butter, softened

DIRECTIONS
…*Cook sugar, yolks, and lemon juice over low heat, stirring constantly.*
…*Cook until mixture thickens and coats a spoon (Do not boil.)*
…*Remove from heat.*
…*Beat in butter and lemon rind.*
…*Chill.*
(May be made up to a week before serving.)

Uses:
Put in a pie/tart crust.
Top with strawberries, raspberries, or blueberries.
Serve with whipped cream.

LIME PINE SALAD/DESSERT

INGREDIENTS
8 oz. cream cheese
8 oz. whipped topping
8 oz. crushed pineapple
Two 3 oz. boxes lime gelatin
1 c. chopped pecans
2 c. marshmallows

DIRECTIONS
...Soften cream cheese.
...Add whipped topping,
pineapple, and gelatin (which
has been dissolved with
marshmallows in 1 c. hot
water).
...Stir in nuts.
...Pour into mold and refrigerate
for 4 hours.

PARTY LEMON ICE

INGREDIENTS
2 c. water
3 c. sugar
1 1/4 c. lemon juice
2 tsp. lemon rind
1/4 tsp. salt
8 c. water

DIRECTIONS
...Combine 2 c. of water and
sugar in a saucepan.
...Bring to a boil.
...Chill in refrigerator before
adding remaining ingredients.
...Freeze in electric freezer.

PIE CRUST

INGREDIENTS
4 c. flour
1 3/4 c. vegetable shortening
1 Tbsp. sugar
2 tsp. salt
1 Tbsp. vinegar
1 egg
1/2 c. water

DIRECTIONS
...Sift flour, sugar, and salt.
...With pastry blender or fork,
mix in shortening.
...In a separate small bowl, mix
vinegar, egg, and water.
...Stir the two mixtures with a
fork until blended together.
...Chill at least 15 minutes before
rolling.
...Freezes well.
(Dough may be kept in
refrigerator up to 3 days.)
Makes 4 to 5 double crust pies.

PISTACHIO DESSERT

INGREDIENTS
35 Ritz crackers, crushed
3/4 c. butter
2 packages instant gelatin
  pistachio pudding
1 1/2 c. milk
1 qt. vanilla ice cream
Frozen dessert topping
2 Heath bars

DIRECTIONS
…Melt butter and crackers for
crust.
…Spread into a 9x13 casserole and
bake for 7 minutes at 350 degrees.
…Let cool.
…Beat pudding, milk, and ice
cream.
…Pour over crust and freeze.
…Top with frozen dessert topping
and crushed Heath Bars just
before serving.

PRETZEL SALAD/ DESSERT

INGREDIENTS
2 c. crushed pretzels
1 1/2 sticks margarine, melted
1/4 c. sugar
8 oz. cream cheese, softened
1 c. sugar
6 oz. box strawberry gelatin
1 1/2 c. frozen dessert topping
One 20 oz. can crushed pineapple,
  drained with juice reserved
Two 10 oz. packages frozen
  strawberries, thaw and drain
  well reserving juice

DIRECTIONS
…Mix pretzels, margarine, and 1/2 c.
sugar.
…Press into 9x13 casserole.
…Bake at 350 degrees for 10 minutes.
…Cool.
…Mix cream cheese and 1 c. sugar.
…Add frozen dessert topping.
…Spread over crust.
…Dissolve gelatin in juices and add
enough water to equal 2 cups.
…Heat gelatin and refrigerate until
syrupy.
…Add pineapple and strawberries and
spread over cream cheese.
…Chill.

Raising Bi-Racial Children ~ When my husband, a black neurosurgeon, decided to take a job in Topeka, KS, moving our family from San Francisco, I was more than a little nervous. This was after all the town of the landmark court ruling against school segregation, Brown vs. Board of Education. It turned out that race was less an issue for us than our children. Although we were the only bi-racial couple on the block, we were warmly embraced by our white, mostly conservative neighbors. So it was a shock to us when our boys encountered open racism in grade school, which grew worse when they were old enough to start dating, more because of the parents than the girls themselves. The racism manifested itself in some unhappy romantic break-ups. In these situations, there was nothing for us as parents to do but to love our children as much and as openly as we could. Strength to face the trials of the world begins at home inside the family. We made sure to raise our boys to be proud of both their parent's racial heritages. And they seem to have weathered the rough waters of childhood quite well. Mary Powell Yorke

FOCUS ON YOUNG ADULTHOOD ~ Many mothers think toddlers need the most attention, and this may be true as far as basic needs are concerned, but I believe our children have a greater need for their parents' emotional support as they are developing into young adults. My middle daughter struggled academically during her first couple of years of college. I suggested that she might want to change majors, but she insisted this was what she wanted to do. I said that if she were really serious about her major, she would have to study much harder. I tried to do whatever I could to encourage her and provide support. She was able to get her grades back up and went on to complete a master's degree in the same subject. Kansas State Representative LANA GORDON

PICKY EATERS ~ I did not want my children to be picky eaters. To avoid this, I consciously tried to expose them to as many diverse foods as possible when they were toddlers. They did not eat from the "children's menu," so they did not learn to expect chicken fingers, grilled cheese sandwiches, or cheese pizzas when we dined out. My husband and I would give them, when they were younger, food from our entrees at restaurants. They now enjoy a wide variety of ethnic foods like Indian, Thai, and other Asian cuisines. It is comforting to know that my children will not be picky eaters when they are with other families. KATY FRANKLIN

RASPBERRY TARTS

INGREDIENTS
1 c. butter
6 oz. cream cheese
2 c. flour
Raspberry preserves

DIRECTIONS
…Blend butter, cream cheese, and flour.
…Refrigerate mix for 1 to 2 hours.
…Roll into small balls and press a thumb print into the middle of each ball.
…Bake at 425 degrees for 10 to 12 minutes.
…Before serving, fill with raspberry preserves.

RASPBERRY-AMARETTO SUNDAE

INGREDIENTS
1 pt. raspberry sherbet, softened
1/2 c. sliced almonds
1/4 c. powdered sugar
1/4 c. Amaretto liqueur
1 c. heavy cream

Sauce
One 10 oz. pkg. frozen raspberries, thawed reserving juice
1 tsp. lemon juice
1 tsp. corn starch
3 Tbsp. Amaretto

DIRECTIONS
…Blend sherbet, almonds, sugar, and Amaretto.
…Whip cream to stiff peaks and fold into sherbet mixture.
…Freeze in 4x8x3 loaf pan for 1 day.
(May be kept in freezer, covered, for 1 to 2 months.)
Serves 6 to 8

…Sauce may be prepared several hours or several days before serving.
…Drain berry juice into small saucepan.
…Add lemon juice and bring to a boil.
…Blend cornstarch with 1 Tbsp. water.
…Add to juice and stir until thickened.
…Remove from heat.
…Add berries.
…Stir in Amaretto.
…Serve at room temperature.
…Pour over individual slice of sherbet.
…Garnish with fresh mint if desired.

STRAWBERRIES SABAYON

INGREDIENTS
3 egg yolks
3 oz. granulated sugar
3/4 c. wine or champagne
2 pints strawberries

DIRECTIONS
…Beat egg yolks and sugar in stainless steel bowl until light and fluffy.
…Add wine or champagne.
…Place over simmering water.
…Continue to whip constantly until mixture is hot and thick enough to coat a spoon.
…Serve immediately over strawberries, other berries or fruit. Serves 4 to 6.

SUGAR COOKIE-RAISIN TARTS

INGREDIENTS
1 c. butter
3 eggs
1 tsp. vanilla
1 tsp. baking powder
1/4 tsp. salt
1 1/4 c. sugar

Filling
2 c. raisins
1/2 c. sugar
1 Tbsp. tapioca
1 1/4 c. water
1 tsp. vanilla

DIRECTIONS
…Sift baking powder, salt, and sugar.
…Add butter and mix like a meal.
…Add eggs and vanilla.
…Mixture will be very stiff.
…Cover and chill.

Filling
…In a saucepan, mix raisins, sugar, tapioca, and water.
…Add vanilla.
…Roll chilled dough and cut with round cookie cutter.
…Place cookies on a baking sheet.
…Top each with a Tbsp. of raisin mixture and top with another cookie.
…Crimp edges.
…Prick the top with a fork and bake until edges are brown in 350 degree oven.
(Freezes very well.)

THEO LANDON'S DESSERT

INGREDIENTS
1 c. chopped dates
1 tsp. soda
1 1/4 c. boiling water
3/4 c. shortening
1 c. sugar
2 eggs
1 tsp. vanilla
1 1/2 c. flour
1/2 tsp. salt
1 c. chocolate chips
1/2 c. sugar
Whipped cream
  for topping

DIRECTIONS
...Combine dates and soda.
...Pour boiling water over dates.
...Let cool.
...Cream shortening and sugar.
...Add eggs.
...Then add vanilla.
...Add flour and salt alternately with date mixture.
...Pour into 9x13 greased casserole.
...Sprinkle 1 c. chocolate chips and 1/2 c. sugar over the top.
...Bake 35 to 40 minutes.
...Serve with whipped cream.

(Mrs. Landon was the wife of Alf Landon, former governor of Kansas and 1936 Republican candidate for President of the United States.)

WASH-DAY COBBLER

INGREDIENTS
1 c. butter
1 c. self-rising flour
1 c. sugar
1 c. milk
1 qt. fresh or canned fruit

DIRECTIONS
...Melt butter in a 9x13 pan.
...Combine flour, sugar, and milk.
...Pour over butter.
...Spread fruit over the top.
...Bake at 350 degrees for 40 minutes.
...Serve warm with ice cream or dessert topping.
(In pioneer days when the housewife spent all day on laundry, this was a quick dessert, hence the name.)

200 / Cookies & bars

Cookies & bars

TWO TO TANGO ~ One of the most useful things I believe our parents taught my sibling and I was, "It takes two to tango." Any time there was a disagreement/argument, we were not allowed to "blame" someone else for our own actions. If there was an argument, obviously two sides had participated. The saying taught us many lessons that I am still using as a parent and am trying to pass on to my children. Not only taking responsibility for what you say and do, but also remembering that if you are angry with someone, it is very likely they are angry with you. JANA BARRY

THE MONEY TREE ~ Why do so many children expect financial assistance beyond their college graduation? Sure, the economy plays a part in this, but studies suggest that grown children expect and many receive money beyond the scope of the last generation. Young adults are moving back home at an alarming rate. Grandparents in large numbers are raising another generation of children. A judge, who has seen it all from the bench, suggested this analogy: "Every family has a money tree. In some families there is a lot of money on the tree. In others just a little. But the kids will come and take the money until it is gone." Parents must decide when enough is enough because children will not do it for them. In our family the kids are on their own. What they earn is what they can spend. LINDA POLLY

COOKIES

AMISH SUGAR COOKIES

INGREDIENTS
1 c. sugar
1 c. powdered sugar
1 c. butter
1 c. oil
2 eggs
4 1/2 c. flour
1 tsp. baking soda
1 tsp. cream of tartar
1 tsp. vanilla

DIRECTIONS
…Combine sugars, butter, and oil.
…Beat well.
…Add eggs.
…Beat again.
…Drop small balls of dough on a cookie sheet.
…Flatten slightly with a fork that has been dipped in sugar.
…Bake at 375 degrees for 10 to 12 minutes.

APRICOT BALLS

INGREDIENTS
8 oz. dried apricots, ground or chopped
2 1/2 c. flaked coconut
2/3 c. finely chopped nuts
3/4 c. sweetened condensed milk

DIRECTIONS
…Mix apricots, coconut, and milk together.
…Roll into one-inch balls.
…Roll balls in nuts.
…Let stand two hours or until firm.

APRICOT SQUARES

INGREDIENTS
1 1/2 c. sifted flour
1 c. brown sugar
1 tsp. baking powder
1 1/2 c. quick cooking oats
3/4 c. butter or margarine
1 1/2 c. apricot jam

DIRECTIONS
…Mix flour, baking powder, brown sugar, and oats together.
…Cut in butter or margarine until crumbly.
…Pat 2/3 of mixture into a 9x13 pan.
…Spread jam onto mixture.
…Cover with remaining crumb mixture.
…Bake at 350 degrees for about 30 minutes.
…Watch closely.
…Cool.
…Cut into squares.

BLUE RIBBON SUGAR COOKIES

INGREDIENTS
1 1/2 c. flour
1/2 tsp. baking powder
1/2 tsp. salt
1/2 c. butter
1/2 c. sugar
1 egg
2 Tbsp. milk
1 tsp. lemon extract

DIRECTIONS
…Cream butter and sugar.
…Add egg.
…Slowly add dry ingredients alternately with milk and lemon extract.
…Blend well and chill several hours.
…Roll dough on a floured surface.
…Cut into shapes and bake at 350 degrees for 7 to 10 minutes.
…Makes 1 1/2 dozen cookies.

BUTTER THINS

INGREDIENTS
2 c. butter
3 1/2 c. powdered sugar
5 eggs, well beaten
4 c. sifted flour
1 tsp. baking soda dissolved in
   1/2 c. sour cream
1 tsp. vanilla
1/4 tsp. salt

DIRECTIONS
…Cream butter and powdered sugar.
…Add eggs, then flour.
…Stir in soda dissolved in sour cream, vanilla and salt.
…Mix well.
…Chill.
…Roll out very thin on a floured board and cut into shapes.
…Bake on a greased cookie sheet at 350 degrees for 10 minutes. (Frost for extra rich cookie.)
Makes 100 cookies.

IF I COULD DO IT OVER ~

I regret we didn't have a family pet until my three children (Eric, Jennifer, and Allison) were much older. In retrospect, I now realize the pleasure, company, solace, unconditional love, and sheer stress relief a pet brings would have been wonderful for them as small children. Disappointments in school and hurt feelings from insensitive playmates could have been somewhat alleviated with the stroke of a furry paw. MARILYN UNREIN

CHOCOLATE CHIP
ICE CREAM SANDWICHES

INGREDIENTS
1 1/4 c. flour
1/2 tsp. soda
1/2 tsp. salt
1/2 c. butter
1/2 c. brown sugar
1/4 c. sugar
1 egg
3/4 tsp. vanilla
1 c. mini-chocolate chips
1/2 gallon vanilla ice cream

DIRECTIONS
…Sift soda, salt, and flour
in bowl.
…In mixer bowl, beat butter for
30 seconds.
…Add sugars and beat until
fluffy.
…Add egg and vanilla and beat
well.
…Add dry ingredients, beating
until well mixed.
…Stir in chocolate chips.
…Drop dough by teaspoonful
2 inches apart onto ungreased
cookie sheet.
…Bake at 375 degrees 8 to 10
minutes.
…For cookie sandwiches, place
a small scoop of ice cream on the
flat side of one cookie.
…Top with second cookie.
…Freeze until ready to eat.

CHOCOLATE
PECAN COOKIES

INGREDIENTS
1 c. sugar
1 egg
2 squares melted chocolate
1/4 c. butter
1/2 c. flour
1 tsp. vanilla
1 c. chopped pecans

DIRECTIONS
…Mix sugar, egg, chocolate, butter,
flour, vanilla, and pecans.
…With a teaspoon make little
walnut sized heaps on a greased
cookie sheet.
…Bake at 300 degrees for 6 to 8
minutes.
…Press 1/2 pecan into each cookie
while still warm.
Makes 3 dozen.
(Recipe doubles easily.)

DOUBLE CHOCOLATE DROPS

INGREDIENTS

One 12 oz. package
  chocolate chips
1 c. shortening
1 c. sugar
2 eggs
2 tsp. vanilla
2 c. flour
1 tsp. soda
1 tsp. salt
1 c. chopped pecans

DIRECTIONS

...Put 1/3 of the chocolate
bits in a double boiler and
melt.
...Cream shortening and
sugar. Stir into unbeaten eggs
and cool melted chocolate.
...Add dry ingredients.
...Stir in nuts and remaining
chocolate chips.
...Drop by teaspoon onto
ungreased cookie sheet.
...Bake at 375 degrees for 8 to
10 minutes.
Makes 3 dozen cookies.

GUMDROP COOKIES _____

INGREDIENTS

1 lb. spiced gum drops
1/2 lb. raisins
1/2 c. chopped pecans
1 c. flour
1/2 c. butter
1/2 c. sugar
3/4 c. applesauce
1 tsp. cinnamon
1/2 tsp. soda
1/2 tsp. salt
1/2 tsp. ginger
1/2 tsp. cloves
1/2 tsp. nutmeg

DIRECTIONS

...Preheat oven to 300
degrees.
...Cream butter and sugar.
...Add applesauce,
cinnamon, soda, salt,
ginger, cloves, and nutmeg.
...Mix together gum drops,
raisins, pecans, and flour.
...Add to butter mixture.
...Drop by teaspoon onto
cookie sheet.
...Bake at 300 degrees for
15 minutes.

PARENT VS. FRIEND ~ Love
your children, but don't
try to be a friend until
they are on their own.
JANET MCELROY

ICEBOX COOKIES

INGREDIENTS

1 1/2 c. butter
1 c. sugar
1 c. brown sugar
3 eggs, beaten
4 1/2 c. flour
2 tsp. soda
1 tsp. cinnamon
1 tsp. cloves
1 c. walnuts, finely chopped

DIRECTIONS

…Cream butter and sugars.
…Add eggs, then all other ingredients.
…Form into rolls 1 1/2 inch thick.
…Wrap in waxed paper and refrigerate for several hours.
…Slice 1/8 inch thick and bake at 350 degrees for 10 to 12 minutes.
…Cool and store in air tight container.

KORNY KANSAS COOKIES

INGREDIENTS

1 1/4 c. yellow cornmeal
1 1/2 c. flour
1 c. sugar
1/2 tsp. soda
1/2 tsp. salt
1 c. butter
1 egg, beaten
1 tsp. vanilla
Whole pecans

DIRECTIONS

…In a mixing bowl, combine cornmeal, flour, sugar, soda, and salt.
…Cut the butter in with a fork or pastry blender until mixture is crumbly.
…Add egg and vanilla and mix well.
…Shape dough into 1 inch balls and place 2 inches apart on a greased cookie sheet.
…Place a pecan on top of each cookie and press down.
…Bake at 325 degrees for 15 to 18 minutes.
…Cool on cookie sheet for one minute before removing.
…Makes 4 dozen.

LILLIE BELLE'S OLD TIME OATMEAL COOKIES

INGREDIENTS
2 c. oatmeal
2 c. flour
2 c. sugar
1 1/2 c. margarine or shortening
3 eggs
2 c. raisins
1 pinch salt
2 tsp. baking powder

DIRECTIONS
…Cream shortening and sugar well.
…Add eggs one at a time, beating mixture after each egg.
…Add flour, then oatmeal, then salt and baking powder.
…Drop spoonfuls onto greased cookie sheet.
…Bake at 350 degrees for 10 to 12 minutes.

PECAN TEA BALLS

INGREDIENTS
1 c. butter
4 Tbsp. honey
2 c. flour, sifted
1/4 tsp. salt
2 tsp. vanilla
1 c. pecans, chopped
Powdered sugar

DIRECTIONS
…Mix all ingredients in the order listed.
…Chill dough one hour or more.
…Roll into small balls and place on ungreased cookie sheet.
…Bake 10 to 12 minutes at 350 degrees.
…While still warm, roll in powdered sugar.

READING FOR A LIFETIME ~

Our son, Eric, was not motivated to read as a youngster. Since his father had been dyslexic as a youth, we feared this could be a factor for Eric as well. Testing revealed he was not dyslexic, so we began a program of paying him $1.00 for each book he completed. Since he had a very limited allowance, this proved to be a motivator (despite the experts who reject this idea)! After a year or so of collecting dollars for books read, Eric announced: "You don't have to pay me to read anymore. I like to read." And read he did, through a Ph.D. in Ancient Semitic Languages and a book published in 2004.

PAT REYMOND

POWDERED SUGAR COOKIES

INGREDIENTS
1 1/2 c. sugar, sifted
1 c. butter (use part shortening for firmer cookie)
1 egg
1 tsp. vanilla
1/2 tsp. almond flavoring
2 1/2 c. flour
1 tsp. soda
1 tsp. cream of tartar

DIRECTIONS
…Heat oven to 375 degrees.
…Beat sugar and butter.
…Add egg, vanilla, and almond flavoring.
…Mix well.
…Sift flour with other dry ingredients.
…Blend into sugar mixture.
…Refrigerate 2 to 3 hours.
…Roll out on lightly floured board and cut into shapes.
…Bake for 8 to 10 minutes. (Watch closely.)

VARIATIONS

Cookie Puppets: Cut out with patterns traced from story books or cookie cutters.

Egg Yolk Paint: Mix 1 egg yolk and 1/4 tsp. water. Divide mixture into small containers. Tint each with a different food color. If "paint" thickens while standing, stir in a few drops of water. Press cut out cookie lightly onto wooden skewers. Bake and decorate.

Paintbrush Cookies: Prepare egg yolk paint. Paint designs (flowers, plaids, strips, etc.) on cookies with small paint brushes. You can paint before or after baking.

SINFUL CHOCOLATE CHUNK COOKIES

INGREDIENTS

Two 8 oz. packages semi-sweet
   baking chocolate
3/4 c. brown sugar
1/4 c. butter, softened
2 eggs
1 1/2 tsp. vanilla
1 tsp. instant coffee crystals
1/2 c. flour (if omitting nuts,
   increase flour to 3/4 c.)
1/4 tsp. baking powder
2 c. chopped nuts

DIRECTIONS

…Preheat oven to 350 degrees.
…Coarsely chop 8 oz. chocolate.
…Microwave remaining 8 oz.
chocolate on high for 2 minutes.
…Stir until chocolate is melted.
…Stir in sugar, butter, eggs, and
vanilla with a spoon until well
blended.
…Stir in coffee, flour, and baking
powder.
…Stir in chopped chocolate and
nuts.
…Drop by 1/4 cupful onto
ungreased cookie sheet.
…Bake 13 to 14 minutes or until
set.
…Cool on cookie sheet 1 minute.
…Transfer to wire rack and cool
completely.
Makes 18 large cookies.

SNICKERDOODLES

INGREDIENTS

1 1/2 c. sugar
1 c. shortening
2 eggs
1 tsp. vanilla
2 3/4 c. flour
1 tsp. soda
2 tsp. cream of tartar
1/2 tsp. salt
1 c. sugar mixed with 1/4 c.
   cinnamon.

DIRECTIONS

…Cream sugar, shortening, eggs,
and vanilla.
…Sift flour, soda, cream of tartar,
and salt, and fold into shortening
mixture.
…Roll into balls the size of a walnut.
…Roll ball in a mixture of sugar
and cinnamon.
…Bake on an ungreased cookie
sheet at 350 degrees for about 10
minutes or until light brown, but
still soft in the middle.
…Do not over bake.

SUGAR COOKIES

INGREDIENTS
1/2 c. margarine
1/2 c. shortening
1 c. sugar
1 egg
1 tsp. vanilla
2 1/2 c. flour
1 tsp. soda

DIRECTIONS
…Cream margarine, shortening, sugar, and egg.
…Add vanilla and mix well.
…Combine flour and soda and add to creamed mixture.
…Drop onto cookie sheet two inches apart.
…Flatten with the bottom of a glass dipped in water and sugar.
…Bake at 375 degrees for 10 minutes.

"DANCE, as if no one were watching, sing as if no one were listening, and live as if it were your last day."
IRISH PROVERB

ENJOY THEM EVERY DAY ~ These words of wisdom are so true. I do not have a degree in motherhood and sometimes in my search to earn the "Best Mom" award, I forget the simple stuff — to love and enjoy my family each and every day! When my children were babies and I often felt overwhelmed, wise women reminded me to "Relax and enjoy them now, for they grow up quickly!" With both of our children racing through school, we are living the "quick" part of life. I am still a "work in progress" but I am striving daily to relax and enjoy all that life brings. May you, too, Dance, Sing, and Live! DORI MURPHY

BARS

BEST BROWNIES

--from Kansas Governor
Kathleen Sebelius

INGREDIENTS
8 oz. unsweetened chocolate
3/4 lb. butter
6 eggs
3 c. sugar
3 Tbsp. vanilla
1 1/2 c. flour
1 1/2 c. pecans

DIRECTIONS
…Melt chocolate and butter.
…Cream eggs with sugar and
vanilla.
…Add chocolate and butter.
…Mix flour and nuts and add
to other mixture.
…Pour into greased and floured
8x8 pan.
…Bake at 350 degrees for 30 minutes.

MOM FOREVER ~ I know no matter how old my children are I will never stop worrying or praying or mothering. Whether it is food for a celebration, a homecoming, or sharing a family recipe over the phone, the tastes of home are always a comfort. PAULA O'CALLAGHAN

CARAMEL BARS

INGREDIENTS
One 12 oz. bag caramels
6 Tbsp. milk
1 c. oatmeal
1 c. flour
1/2 tsp. soda
3/4 c. sugar
1/2 tsp. salt
3/4 c. melted butter
1 c. chocolate chips
1/2 c. chopped nuts

DIRECTIONS
...Melt caramels and milk in a double boiler.
...Cool.
...Mix oatmeal, flour, soda, sugar, salt, and butter until crumbly.
...Press 1/2 of mixture into a greased 9x13 casserole dish.
...Bake at 325 degrees for 10 minutes.
...Sprinkle on chocolate chips and nuts.
...Drizzle caramel mixture over the top.
...Top with remaining half of crumbs for the crust.
...Bake an additional 20 to 25 minutes.

FUDGE SCOTCH SQUARES

INGREDIENTS
1 1/2 c. graham cracker crumbs
1 can sweetened condensed milk
1 c. chocolate chips
1 c. butterscotch chips
1 c. chopped walnuts

DIRECTIONS
...Mix all ingredients well.
...Press mixture into very well-greased 9 inch square pan.
...Bake at 350 degrees for 30 to 35 minutes.
...Cool for 45 minutes.
...Cut into squares.

GOOD OLE DAYS PECAN BARS

INGREDIENTS

Crust

*1 package yellow cake
mix (remove 2/3 c. for
filling)*

1/2 c. butter

1 egg

Filling

2/3 c. cake mix

*1/2 c. packed brown
sugar*

*1 c. chopped pecans
for topping*

1 tsp. vanilla

3 eggs

DIRECTIONS

*…Grease sides and bottom of
a 9x13 pan.*

*…Mix crust ingredients until
crumbly.*

…Press into bottom of pan.

*…Bake at 350 degrees for 15 to
20 minutes (glass pan at 325
degrees) until golden brown.*

*…Mix filling ingredients
except pecans, at medium
speed until smooth.*

…Pour over crust.

…Top with pecans.

*…Bake for 30 to 35 additional
minutes until filling sets.*

…Cool.

…Cut into bars.

HEARTLAND YUMMY BARS

INGREDIENTS

1/4 lb. butter, melted

1 c. graham cracker crumbs

1 c. coconut

1 c. chocolate chips

1 c. butterscotch chips

1 c. walnuts or pecans, chopped

*One 14 oz. can sweetened
condensed milk*

DIRECTIONS

*…Melt butter in a 9x13 pan and
layer in order the remaining
ingredients.*

*…Bake at 350 degrees for 25 to 30
minutes.*

…Cut into bars.

LEMON BARS

INGREDIENTS
1 c. butter
1/2 c. powdered sugar
2 c. flour
1/2 tsp. salt
4 eggs
6 Tbsp. flour
2 c. sugar
6 Tbsp. lemon juice
1 tsp. grated lemon rind

DIRECTIONS
…Mix butter, powdered sugar, flour, and salt and press into 9x13 greased pan.
…Bake at 350 degrees for 20 minutes.
…Beat thoroughly eggs, flour, sugar, lemon juice and lemon rind.
…Spread over warm pastry.
…Bake at 350 degrees for 25 minutes.
…Immediately sprinkle with powdered sugar.
…Cool and cut into 1 or 2 inch squares.

NANA'S BUTTER BARS

INGREDIENTS
1/2 c. butter, melted and
  partially cooled
3 eggs
1 box yellow cake mix
One 1 lb. package powdered sugar
One 8 oz. package cream cheese
Salt
Vanilla

DIRECTIONS
…Beat butter, 1 egg, and cake mix with electric mixer until crumbly.
…Spread into bottom of 9x13 pan.
…Beat 2 eggs, powdered sugar, and cream cheese for 5 minutes.
…Add small amounts of salt and vanilla.
…Pour over cake mixture.
…Bake at 350 degrees for 30 to 35 minutes.
…Cut into bars when cool.

WORK VS. PLAY ~

I tell my kids that school is their "job" and that all sports and extracurricular activities are a privilege. If they do not get good grades or act appropriately at school, no extras!

KAREN TROBOUGH

SPECIAL K BARS

INGREDIENTS
1 c. white sugar
1 c. light corn syrup
1 1/2 c. creamy peanut
    butter
6 c. Special K cereal
One 12 oz. package
    butterscotch chips
One 12 oz. package
    chocolate chips.

DIRECTIONS
…Heat sugar and syrup
over medium heat until
mixture reaches a boil.
…Remove from heat and
add peanut butter.
…Stir in cereal until
evenly coated.
…Spread mixture into a
greased 9x13 casserole.
…Melt butterscotch and
chocolate chips together in
microwave until creamy.
…Spread evenly over
cereal mixture and cool.
…Cut into bars.
No baking required.

TOFFEE BARS

INGREDIENTS
1 c. butter
1 c. brown sugar
1 egg yolk
1 c. flour
6 chocolate candy bars
Nuts

DIRECTIONS
…Cream butter, brown sugar,
and egg yolk.
…Add flour and spread into
a 9x13 pan.
…Bake at 325 degrees for 10
to 15 minutes or until edges
start to brown.
…Layer candy over top while
hot and spread when melted.
…Top with nuts.

TRUST YOUR INSTINCTS ~

I believe as a mother that I know my children better than anyone else, and I have learned to trust my instincts when something doesn't seem quite right. Once I had a feeling my daughter had strep throat. The doctor tried to make me feel like I didn't know what I was talking about, but I insisted he test her. The throat culture proved my suspicions were correct. This experience taught me to be strong enough to trust my natural mothering instincts when it comes to my children and never let an "expert" intimidate me again.

Kansas State Representative LANA GORDON

VANILLA BROWNIES

INGREDIENTS
1 c. butter
2 c. sugar
4 eggs
2 c. flour
1/2 tsp. salt
1 tsp. vanilla

Frosting
1/3 c. butter
3 Tbsp. cream
3 c. powdered sugar
1 1/2 tsp. vanilla

DIRECTIONS
...Cream sugar and butter.
...Add eggs one at a time.
...Add vanilla, then flour and salt that have been mixed together.
...Pour into greased 9x13 pan.
...Bake 25 to 30 minutes at 350 degrees.

Frosting
...Cream butter. Add sugar, cream, and vanilla.
...Add a few drops of yellow food coloring if desired.

EXTRAS EXTRAS EXTRAS EXTRAS EXTRAS EXTRAS EXTRAS EXTRAS EXTRAS EXTRAS EXTRAS E

Extras

Extras   *Extras*

EXTRAS EXTRAS

WORDS OF WISDOM ~ There is nothing wrong with your children that twenty years won't cure.

A mother is only as happy as her saddest child.

There are two things a mother can give a child. One is roots and the other is wings.

The time you like your children the least is when they need your love the most.

BABY #2 ~ The arrival of my second child was exhausting. Along with all the added work, one of the hardest things to deal with was that all the attention being paid to the baby makes the first feel ignored. I anticipated this and bought inexpensive little books and toys for our four-year-old throughout my pregnancy, wrapped them, and hid them in the closet. I remember the day two packages arrived for his new baby sister, and our son burst into tears. I immediately took him to the "present closet" and pulled out some small gifts just for him. We did this several times in the next few months, and he was so delighted that he never thought about how the mailman got those packages into the closet. When I take a present to a new baby, I always remember the older child with a small toy or book. LINDA POLLY

APPLESAUCE

INGREDIENTS
2 lbs. tart apples
1/4 c. water
1/4 c. sugar
1/4 tsp. cinnamon (optional)

DIRECTIONS
…Core apples and cut them
into quarters.
…Do not peel.
…Place them in a large pot.
…Add the water and cover.
…Cook over low heat until
the apples are tender, about
20 minutes.
…Pulse apples in a food
processor until chunky, not
pureed.
…Cook again over low heat
for 5 to 10 minutes.
…Add cinnamon.
…Serve hot or cold.

CASHEW-RAISIN CLUSTERS

INGREDIENTS
1 c. raisins
1 lb. salted cashews
1 lb. chocolate bark

DIRECTIONS
…Steam raisins over boiling
water for 5 minutes.
…Let raisins stand for several
hours until completely dry.
…Melt chocolate bark and stir in
raisins and cashews.
…Drop by teaspoon onto waxed
paper and allow to cool.
(You may refrigerate and also
substitute white chocolate bark
for the dark.)

APPLE BUTTER

INGREDIENTS
1 gal. applesauce
6 c. sugar
5 tsp. cinnamon
1 tsp. allspice
3/4 tsp. cloves

DIRECTIONS
…Bring all ingredients to a boil.
…Cook 15 minutes.
…Lower heat and simmer for
30 minutes.

TIME OUTS ~ I discovered that "time outs" for bad behavior work best when you give your children a kitchen minute timer and let them set it. This way they know themselves when the "time out" has ended. NANCY KINDLING

CINNAMON BUTTER

INGREDIENTS
1 lb. butter, softened
1 Tbsp. ground cinnamon

DIRECTIONS
…Beat butter until fluffy.
…Blend in cinnamon.
…Serve at room temperature.

CITRUS TEA PUNCH

INGREDIENTS
2 tea bags
1 c. boiling water
3/4 c. sugar
1 1/2 c. fresh orange juice
1 c. lemon juice
1/4 c. Grenadine syrup
One 12 oz. bottle ginger ale

DIRECTIONS
…Steep tea.
…Add sugar until dissolved.
…Add all other ingredients.
(May add liquor of your choice to make into a cocktail, usually champagne or vodka.)

COCOA MIX

INGREDIENTS
One 2 lb. box instant chocolate drink mix
1 lb. jar dairy creamer
One 8 qt. size box powdered skim milk
2 c. powdered sugar, sifted

DIRECTIONS
…Mix the four ingredients together and store in tightly covered containers.
…To use, mix in a cup 1 part mix to 2 parts boiling water.

COUNTRY RHUBARB JAM

INGREDIENTS
5 c. rhubarb (fresh or frozen),
  cut in small pieces
3 c. sugar
One 3 oz. box raspberry
  flavored gelatin

DIRECTIONS
...Simmer rhubarb and sugar
for 20 minutes or until it is a
sauce consistency.
...Do not add water.
...Remove from heat and stir
in gelatin powder.
...Pour into sterilized jelly
glasses with lids.
...Refrigerate.

FOOLPROOF DARK CHOCOLATE FUDGE

INGREDIENTS
3 c. semi-sweet chocolate chips
One 14 oz. can sweetened
  condensed milk
1 c. chopped nuts
1 1/2 tsp. vanilla
Pinch of salt

DIRECTIONS
...In a heavy saucepan melt
chocolate chips, condensed milk
and salt.
...Stir in nuts and vanilla.
...Spread mixture into 8 inch
greased square pan.
...Chill 2 hours or until firm.
(This recipe can be varied by
using white chocolate chips or
butterscotch chips.)

HOLIDAY NUTS

INGREDIENTS
1 c. sugar
1 tsp. cinnamon
1/4 tsp. salt
6 Tbsp. milk
1 tsp. vanilla
2 1/2 c. pecans

DIRECTIONS
...Cook sugar, cinnamon, salt,
and milk to soft ball stage (236
degrees).
...Remove from stove and add
vanilla and nuts.
...Stir until creamy.
...Turn out on waxed paper to
cool.
...Separate.

FINDING HIS OWN PATH ~

Our son completed college as an English major and then went on to graduate studies in Ancient Semitic Languages, earning a Ph.D. from the University of Chicago. When I asked him why he chose this unusual area of interest, he replied, "I wanted to be an expert in something my father is NOT!" His father is both a physicist and a physician, as well as an inventor and an Egyptologist. It was no easy thing for our son to find his own field of interest in which to become an expert! But it was important for him to differentiate himself from his father. I believe it is important to let your children find their own path. PAT REYMOND

WHEN 'NO' IS SOMETIMES BETTER THAN 'YES' ~

While raising my daughters, one of the hardest questions for me to answer was, "When should I say 'no'?" My husband believes a parent should pick his battles and not fight over the little things. If one of our daughters asked to do something that was not harmful to her, Craig always said "yes." It was not that simple for me. Often I would have to listen for a waver in their voice as they asked. If my girls sounded hesitant about asking to stay overnight at a friend's house, or to come home later than their usual curfew, I would often follow my gut feeling and say "no." Sometimes I would see the relief in their eyes immediately that I had said the "no" they were unable to say to their friends themselves. Sometimes it was much later that I found out the innocent overnight or late curfew included not-so-innocent activities that my daughters did not want to be a part of, but did not have the strength to say so. I think listening hard to what my daughters are really asking me is one of the best parenting lessons they have taught me. ROBIN MAXON

HONEY BUTTER

INGREDIENTS
1 lb. butter, softened
1/2 c. honey

DIRECTIONS
…Beat butter until fluffy.
…Blend in honey.
…Serve at room temperature.
(Good with hot wheat bread.)

HOT WASSAIL

INGREDIENTS
1 gal. apple cider
2 tea bags
2 tsp. whole allspice
2 1/2 sticks cinnamon
2/3 c. brown sugar
2 tsp. cloves
1 orange, sliced

DIRECTIONS
…Mix all ingredients except
orange slices and cloves.
…Bring to a boil.
…Reduce heat and simmer 30
minutes.
…Add orange slices and cloves
during the last 10 minutes.

This can also be made in a
36 c. coffee pot.
For this method, place all
ingredients in the coffee basket.
Pour cider into the coffee pot
and brew.

ICED LIME PUNCH

INGREDIENTS
Two 6 oz. cans frozen
   limeade
4 c. water
2 c. lemon juice
1 qt. club soda
1 1/2 c. vodka
Pineapple spears
Fresh mint sprigs

DIRECTIONS
…Combine all ingredients
except pineapple and mint.
…Refrigerate until ice cold.
…Serve in tall, chilled
glasses.
…Garnish with pineapple
and mint.

KANSAS SNACK MIX

INGREDIENTS
12 oz. package oyster crackers
10 oz. box small cheese crackers
15 oz. tiny twist pretzels
2 packages low fat microwave popcorn
1/2 c. vegetable oil
1 1/2 tsp. lemon pepper seasoning
1 envelope dry ranch mix

DIRECTIONS
…Pop popcorn and mix with crackers and pretzels.
…Combine oil, seasoning, and ranch mix.
…Drizzle over cracker mixture until evenly coated.
…Bake in large roaster pan for one hour, mixing every 15 minutes, at 200 degrees.
…Store in airtight container.

"KICK-IT-UP" AFTER DINNER DRINK

INGREDIENTS
1 qt. rich ice cream
1 c. milk
3/4 c. Kentucky bourbon
1/4 c. rum or brandy

DIRECTIONS
…Soften ice cream.
…Blend with milk.
…Add bourbon and brandy or rum.

LINDA'S STRAWBERRY JAM

INGREDIENTS
4 c. strawberries, crushed
8 c. sugar
2 boxes pectin

DIRECTIONS
…Wash and cut off stems of strawberries.
…Crush strawberries in food processor leaving small bits of fruit.
…Stir in sugar with strawberries.
…Let stand 10 minutes.
…Stir pectin into 1 1/2 c. water.
…Bring to a boil stirring constantly.
…Boil one minute.
…Stir pectin mixture into fruit.
…Stir until sugar is dissolved and no longer grainy, about 3 minutes.
…Pour into jars.
…Leave 1/2 inch for expansion during freezing.
…Cover.
(Freeze up to one year, or refrigerate for up to three months.)

MAMIE EISENHOWER FUDGE

INGREDIENTS
2 c. chocolate chips
Three 8 oz. bars semi-sweet chocolate
One 8 oz. jar marshmallow crème
2 c. pecans, chopped
4 1/2 c. sugar
1/4 tsp. salt
One 14 oz. can evaporated milk
2 Tbsp. butter

DIRECTIONS
…Combine chocolate chips, chocolate bars, marshmallow creme, and nuts in a bowl.
…Run hot water in sink and set bowl in water.
…Combine sugar, salt, milk, and butter in large saucepan.
…Boil for 6 minutes stirring constantly.
…Pour over chocolate mixture and stir until chocolate is melted.
…Pour into buttered jelly roll pan.
…Cut and serve after it cools.
(Freezes well.)

MARINADE

INGREDIENTS
3/4 c. canola oil
1/3 c. soy sauce
1/4 c. Worcestershire sauce
1 Tbsp. dry mustard
1 Tbsp. seasoned salt
1 tsp. black pepper
1/4 c. red wine vinegar
1 tsp. parsley flakes
2 garlic cloves, crushed
1/4 c. fresh lemon juice

DIRECTIONS
…Combine all ingredients.
…Pour over sirloin beef cubes, chicken breasts, or pork tenderloin.
…Marinate overnight.
…Drain off marinade.
…Grill meat and enjoy.

MIDWEST MARINADE

INGREDIENTS
1/2 c. vegetable oil
3/4 c. soy sauce
1/2 c. lemon juice
1/2 c. Worcestershire sauce
1/4 c. mustard
2 tsp. pepper
2 cloves garlic, minced

DIRECTIONS
…Mix all ingredients together.
…Use to marinate anything (i.e. chicken, steak, tuna, salmon, etc.)

"Children don't always remember what you say to them or often what you do, but they always remember how you make them feel."

"Sometimes we try so hard to give our children all the things we didn't have while growing up that we fail to give them all the things we did have." PAM FERRELL

MUSTARD SAUCE

INGREDIENTS
1 pt. half and half
4 Tbsp. dry mustard
1 c. sugar
1 c. vinegar
2 beaten eggs
2 Tbsp. flour
Salt to taste

DIRECTIONS
...Heat half and half in a double boiler.
...Add eggs to hot mixture slowly (do not boil the mixture.)
...Mix mustard, sugar, and flour together.
...Whisk into liquid.
...Add vinegar.
...Cook for one hour.
...Stir occasionally.
...Cool and pour into storage jars.

PEACH CHUTNEY

INGREDIENTS
4 lbs. fresh peaches, pitted
1 1/2 lb. brown sugar
1/2 c. chopped onion
1/2 lb. raisins
1 c. crystallized ginger
2 Tbsp. white mustard seeds
1 Tbsp. salt
2 Tbsp. chili powder
2 c. wine vinegar

DIRECTIONS
...Pit peaches.
...Put peaches, onions, ginger, and raisins through a food processor.
...Add sugar, wine, vinegar, and spices.
...Pour into glass casserole dish.
...Bake at 300 degrees for 2 to 3 hours.
Makes 4 pints.

PECAN TOFFEE

INGREDIENTS
2 c. chopped pecans
1/2 c. butter
1/2 c. margarine
1 1/2 c. brown sugar
1 c. chocolate chips

DIRECTIONS
…Sprinkle pecans into 9x13 pan.
…Combine butter, margarine, and brown sugar in a heavy saucepan.
…Bring to a boil over medium heat and cook to 300 degrees (hard crack stage), about 10 minutes.
…Pour cooked mixture over pecans.
…Let set a few minutes.
…Sprinkle chocolate chips over the top.
…Cover and let stand a few minutes.
…Spread melted chocolate over toffee.
…Cool for several hours and break into pieces.

PUPPY CHOW

INGREDIENTS
1 c. butter
1 c. peanut butter
2 c. chocolate chips
One 12 oz. box chex cereal
3 c. powdered sugar

DIRECTIONS
…Melt butter, peanut butter, and chocolate chips together over low heat.
…Place cereal in a large bowl.
…Pour chocolate mixture over cereal and mix well.
…Put powdered sugar in a medium-large grocery bag.
…Add cereal and toss until coated.
…Store in an airtight container.

STRAWBERRY BUTTER

INGREDIENTS
1 lb. butter, softened
1/4 c. strawberry preserves

DIRECTIONS
…Beat the butter until fluffy.
…Blend well with strawberry preserves.
…Serve at room temperature.

SUGARED NUTS

INGREDIENTS
2 Tbsp. water or cooking sherry
1 egg white
1 c. sugar
1/2 tsp. salt
1/4 tsp. cinnamon
1/4 tsp. ground cloves
1/4 tsp. allspice
2 1/2 c. pecan halves

DIRECTIONS
…Whisk liquid with egg white.
…Add sugar and seasonings and beat until foamy, but not stiff.
…Add nuts and stir to coat evenly.
…Spread on foil-lined baking sheet.
…Bake at 250 degrees for one hour or until glaze has dried.
…Watch closely at end of cooking to prevent burning.

WHITE TREASURE

INGREDIENTS
1 box chex cereal, any variety
1/2 bag (6 oz.) small stick pretzels
One 10 oz. can peanuts
One 12 oz. bag M&M's candy
Two 16 oz. bags white chocolate
  or vanilla chips.

DIRECTIONS
…Mix cereal, pretzels, nuts, and M&M's in a large bowl.
…Melt chips in a double boiler or in a microwave.
…Be careful not to burn.
…Stir gently into dry ingredients until mixture is evenly coated and dry.

WINTER-WONDER NIGHTCAP

INGREDIENTS
1 oz. brandy
1 oz. Kahlua
1 oz. dark crème de cacao
Coffee to fill 2 mugs
Whipped cream

DIRECTIONS
…Stir ingredients and pour into two mugs.
…Top with whipped cream.

ABOUT THE TYPE:

Recipes are set in Minion Italic, Small Caps & Oldstyle, designed by Robert Slimbach for Adobe Systems, Mountain View, California in 1989.

Recipe titles et al. are set in Lithos, designed by Carol Twombly for Adobe Systems in 1989.

Stories and other narrative matter set in Tekton, designed by David Siegel for Adobe Systems in 1989.

Section titles and page numbers set in Zapfino, designed by Hermann Zapf for Linotype, Bad Homburg, Germany in 1998.